THE PERSON AND THE POLIS

The John Henry Cardinal Newman Lectures

GENERAL EDITOR: *Craig Steven Titus*

The present collection of essays by recognized scholars in the fields of psychology, philosophy, theology, and law presents the work of the inaugural John Henry Cardinal Newman Lecture Series. This Washington-based lecture series is held under the sponsorship of the Institute for the Psychological Sciences and seeks to promote an international conversation among the several disciplines that treat the human person. The Newman lecture series is held annually, and forthcoming volumes will be published with an eye toward building a body of learned discussion that is catholic both in its breadth of research and in its dialogue with contemporary Catholic thought. The published versions appear under the patronage of St. Catherine of Alexandria in order to demonstrate the conviction of those responsible for the Newman lecture series that the human person flourishes only when the Creator of heaven and earth is loved above all things.

The John Henry Cardinal Newman Lectures

VOLUME 1

THE PERSON AND THE POLIS

Faith and Values within the Secular State

EDITED BY *Craig Steven Titus*

The Institute for the Psychological Sciences Press
Arlington, Virginia

Distributed by
The Catholic University of America Press
620 Michigan Avenue, N.E. / 240 Leahy Hall
Washington, D.C. 20064

The paper used in this publication meets the minimum requirements
of American National Standards for Information Science—Perma-
nence of Paper for Printed Library Materials, ANSI Z39.48-1984.
∞

·

LIBRARY OF CONGRESS CATALOGING-IN-PUBLICATION DATA
The person and the polis : faith and values within the secular state /
edited by Craig Steven Titus.
        p. cm. — (The John Henry Cardinal Newman lectures ; v. 1)
        Includes bibliographical references and index.
        ISBN-13: 978-0-9773103-0-2 (pbk. : alk. paper)
        ISBN-10: 0-9773103-0-2 (pbk. : alk. paper)   1. Christianity and
politics—Catholic Church.   2. Christian sociology—
Catholic Church.   3. Christian ethics—Catholic authors.
4. Catholic Church—Doctrines.   I. Titus, Craig Steven, 1959–
II. Series.
        BX1793.P47 2007
        261.5—dc22
                        2006005255

CONTENTS

ACKNOWLEDGMENTS

In the name of the Institute for the Psychological Sciences, I would like to acknowledge the many actors who contributed to making this collection of essays possible. First of all, I would like to recognize the faithful generosity of Gene and Charlotte Zurlo, who have funded the John Henry Cardinal Newman Lecture Series from its inception. Furthermore, because of Prof. Daniel N. Robinson's benevolent sponsorship, the lectures were held at the Cosmos Club (Washington, D.C.), which has continued to offer a fitting ambiance for genteel discussions. The corporate and personal authorities of the Institute for the Psychological Sciences (Arlington, Virginia) have warmly encouraged the publication of these lectures. Angela and David Franks have lent their stylistic eyes to the introduction, and Ellen Coughlin has applied her very able editorial pencil to the whole volume. Dr. David McGonagle, director of the Catholic University of America Press, and his staff have contributed their competent and careful aid in bringing this volume to fruition. Finally, I would like to acknowledge the foresight of Prof. Robinson, who inspired this series; and the commitment and energy of Dean Gladys Sweeney, who mobilized a host of prominent scholars and organized the series and this publication.

Craig Steven Titus

THE PERSON AND THE POLIS

Craig Steven Titus

INTRODUCTION

CAN Christians help save modern society from its slow self-deconstruction? Can freedom and democracy flourish without Christian intelligence in the West? Can the serious academic pursuit of truth, especially in the human sciences, survive in the airless clime of anti-religious relativism?

Even to the ears of believers, even in this supposedly post-secular age, the thrust of such questions comes as something of a shock, so deep runs the separation of faith and reason in the modern mind. But though there is much handwringing over the threat of "Christian fundamentalism" and "theocracy," it is in fact the case that the contribution of Christian intelligence to Western culture cannot be ignored by anyone committed to the scholarly pursuit of truth, concerned for the welfare of the nation, and dedicated to the preservation and advancement of the permanent achievements of the West, above all the recognition of the dignity of the human person. That is, refusal to admit the contribution of Christian intelligence is a type of obscurantism.

This collection of essays involves an interdisciplinary dialogue between renowned specialists in philosophy, jurisprudence, psychology, and theology. These experts address the place of faith and values in the secular state, how the person and the polis are guided by ethics and religion, and how liberty and transcendence interact in human aspirations. And they venture to pursue these questions beyond the confines of academic specialization. The contributors have risked entering into a constructive dialogue in an attempt to attain a deeper understanding of the human person through the integration of insights from practical wisdom and Christian faith. The vision of the human person is of such import for psychology and the other human sciences that empirical studies by themselves are simply insufficient to answer the scientific demands of these disciplines. Of course, these sciences would not exist without empirical research, but the question is: from what context is the data forged and into what context is the data to be integrated? The human sciences cannot progress without some measure of philosophical understanding of the human person and society. In turn, these more philosophical reflections take the finely tuned observations of the empirical sciences as further points for reflection on human potential. The goal of this volume is to advance the cause of the human person and society by thus synthesizing the genuine contributions of the human sciences with an openness to spiritual sources of understanding and practice. Psychology is one of the human sciences of special concern here, and so one hope is that this work of synthesis will especially contribute to furthering philosophical psychology, which can then inform applied and clinical efforts at prevention, education, and therapy. The contributions to this volume converge around several themes: the human person and community, the secular state and religious communities, faith and values, reason and emotions. Such a dialogue is of course ongoing.

Even though the contributors and their essays need little introduction, we can highlight the importance of each contribution with an overview of the ensemble. It should be said that each of the contributors belongs to the first rank of his respective discipline, and yet each has ventured to participate in a more interdisciplinary philosophical dialogue concerning the human person and the polis. Let us begin with a few contextualizing considerations.

Human persons spontaneously seek to understand personal experience, especially as that experience involves interaction with other persons. In this exigent quest for knowledge of self and others, we naturally draw from the wellsprings of reason and faith. We seek the ultimate truth of things and of people. The deep longing for meaning provides the first impetus for the basic belief that speaking of truth and goodness is not, finally, a consoling fiction, a social convention, a sign of human gullibility. Other profound aspirations drive the human spirit in its ethical and social concerns. They manifest our inclination to transform our communities and families and our very selves.

Now though these inclinations for the true, the good, personal growth, and social thriving are universal drives, there are researchers specifically devoted to the intellectual appropriation of this quest to understand human personal and social reality. In addition, more specific ethical and moral matters are the proper—though non-exclusive—domain of philosophers and theologians, who search for knowledge and wisdom about human action through the use of reason and faith. However, the able philosopher and theologian will certainly not ignore the practical wisdom incarnated in common sense, custom, and culture, or the insights into the human psyche found through psychological practice and empirical studies.

The articles that you have in your hands, even the ones not written by professional philosophers and theologians, therefore unfold according to at least a philosophical orientation. Precisely in so doing, they attempt to surmount several weaknesses that have plagued academic approaches to the human sciences in general and to psychology in particular. First of all, this collection's approach offers a viable alternative to the excessive compartmentalization of the sciences. The sciences have tended to develop their own languages, conceptions, and methods whose findings, at the end of the day, do not translate easily for the non-specialist, or even for researchers in other sciences. The human sciences, moreover, have too often adopted a model from the natural sciences that tends toward reductionism and over-extension. On the one hand, there is a propensity to reduce the field of investigation so as to obtain statistically relevant findings, at the expense of oversimplifying and distorting reality. On the other hand, there is a tendency to overstate the applicability of findings. Theories become facts before their time, that is, before they are verified. And areas where verification is impossible give rise to speculation, usually at once materialist, moral, and metaphysical, by sciences that according to their own self-definition have no title to engage in such discourse.

A second weakness of the human sciences when pursued in a philosophically naive way is that they are generally dominated by an anti-religious ideology, one that is reinforced by popularized media presentations. This is devastating for an authentic pursuit of the human sciences, especially given that these media images have tended to misrepresent religion's and theology's contributions to the democratic vision of the human person and society. We have already gotten some sense of how this collection of essays helps in rescuing the human sciences from anti-religious provincialism by opening those sciences up to the free air of spiritual reality. Now let us briefly take up each essay in turn.

A major thrust of this collection is the relationship between faith and reason, as expressed in religion and values and as perceived as a real basis for moral judgments. Kenneth Schmitz's essay, "A Contemporary Philosophy of Action," can be taken as the basis for understanding the whole volume. In order to articulate the human, spiritual, and religious values that underlie the highest form of individual and personal action, Schmitz calls upon a man of action, who was also a philosopher of action, the late Karol Wojtyła, Pope John Paul II. With phenomenological flare, Schmitz traces Wojtyła's life and philosophic reflections, especially concerning the divers types of human action. Beyond distinctions between simple motion, vital action, and conscious action, human action, properly speaking, demands a final motive and a formal means. It requires not only reason, not only the acting mind, but the sensory, emotive, and intelligent complex of the human person in action. Drawing on four sources (culture, prayer, classical philosophy, and contemporary concerns), Wojtyła's thought addresses the new paradigm of action occasioned by current techno-logical progress. First, he appeals to the undercurrents of culture in order not only to develop a "philosophy of the acting person," but also to provide cultural bases for resistance to tyrannical forms of author-ity. Drawing on the person's relationship to the community as the key for understanding human action, he recognizes the influence of cul-ture, art, and religion on the life of the nation. Secondly, he identifies the interior reality of prayer and spirituality in his theory of action. Thirdly, he grounds a metaphysical understanding of the good and the person in classic philosophies concerning the structure of action and moral development. Fourthly, Wojtyła engages in dialogue with the insights and demands of modernity. In particular, he appreciates Husserl's phenomenological method as a means of analyzing the dis-tinctively mental life of the human subject. Influenced by his intellec-tual and pastoral work, Wojtyła's mature analysis of human action is born of a deep understanding of the person, in contact with the world outside and the lived world within. In order to discover the core of free and deliberate human action, he takes a philosophical journey within the human person. The center of this journey is the conscious-ness of our creative capacity for responsible action, where we are clos-est to God in the exercise of religious freedom. It is from this point that we move out to impact the world dramatically. In turn, the world returns to us, shaping who we are and our character. Schmitz empha-sizes that human actions have a distinctively moral quality when in contact with the good, since both knowing and valuing the good in-fluence human acts. It is the good that perfects the human person and that is the ontological basis for natural law, the "ethical law of human nature." Living at the center of the human drama means recognizing that our acts have an urgency, that we can increase or decrease the value of our lives through the internal quality of our human acts. The demand of freedom is that we responsibly engage the given realities of our situation (as artist, entrepreneur, and so on); this freedom is what gives acts their human weight and value. It makes for authentic action that finds direction in the truth of things and in other people as they manifest their genuine value. This contemporary philosophy of action perceives how the truth of human reality demands action that strengthens one's own character, builds the community, and contributes to the world, while daring even to strive for holiness.

Such a philosophy of action is based on a moral realism that has many detractors. However, in Daniel N. Robinson it has an able advocate, as his essay, "In Defense of Moral Realism," demonstrates. Robinson argues that morality is based on "moral properties" that are commonly experienced by all people. He takes to task competing systems of moral discourse, his main foil being moral relativism, which assumes that moral judgments are validly established when based only on human tendencies, cultural and historical factors, or sentiment. Sentimentalist moral theories—so popular in contemporary culture and modern philosophy (as found in, for example, David Hume and Adam Smith)—are one version of this relativism. Although correct moral appraisal arises in part through understanding culture, history, and emotion, Robinson affirms that moral queries ultimately involve reality and have right or wrong answers. Robinson moreover defends morality against reductionist approaches that attempt to substitute the methods of the natural sciences for moral reasoning. In the absence of something more tangible, sentimentalists seek some "intense sense of feeling that is common to the whole species," in the words of David Hume.[1] This approach often conceives of the sentiments, not so much as a window to the soul and to some moral reality beyond themselves, but as the very basis of morality itself: morality as moral sentiment. What could be more evident: being

---

1. David Hume, *An Enquiry Concerning the Principles of Morals,* section 1 (Oxford: Oxford University Press, 1975; original 1751).

angry at injustice, disgusted at infidelity, and so on? However, since sentiments are more a corollary than a cause of morality, Robinson is right to draw on the counterarguments of G. E. Moore to disarm such theories. Indeed, moral sentiment alone cannot provide a foundation for moral theory and principle. Another version of the relativism that Robinson critiques is behaviorism, which maintains, against moral realism, that morality is based on the praise or blame of particular human acts. This position has weak grounding, since its moral ascriptions are rewards and punishment that demand correct knowledge, someone with moral standing, and a shared moral understanding. Morality is thus reduced to a cultural consensus, serving those with the "moral luck" to have been born into a dominant culture and family. In addition to offering critiques of rival moral approaches, Robinson argues for the moral realist position.[2] He addresses the bases: for moral understanding, for the relationship between fact and value and between *is* and *ought,* and for challenging reductionist sciences that would monopolize valid observations about the properties of the world. A major question concerns how such properties—dismantled by scientific method—match with reality as a whole. Robinson reasons that "arguments for moral realism are under no special burden in the matter of non-inferential truth claims." Moral entities neither have the same properties as physical entities, nor need they. Complex wholes—which include not only moral occurrences, such as just acts, but also battles, strategies, and gifts—are no less real for being incompatible with reductionist analyses. This raises metaphysical questions about whether physical terms alone are adequate to describe completely the natural world. Robinson renders us attentive to the sense that we give to moral terms and their capacity to attain the really existing properties of the moral realm.

In the same realist vein, Robert P. George contributes reflections

2. Robinson makes a fuller defense of his position, with constructive arguments, in his noteworthy book *Praise and Blame: Moral Realism and Its Applications* (Princeton, N.J.: Princeton University Press, 2002).

on what might be called legal realism in order to establish "The Concept of Public Morality." He finds in reality a basis for morality, which serves as a basis for understanding and critiquing particular laws. He philosophically addresses major contenders in Anglo-American jurisprudence, such as Ronald Dworkin and John Finnis, concerning the propriety of legislating about moral matters. First, he argues that just as the common good of public health and safety generates obligations in justice (for example, concerning fire threats or toxic pollutants), so the common good of public morality serves as grounds for moral obligations. People have an obligation in justice not to damage the community's moral ecology, that is, not to harm people's moral character or the goods and institutions that depend on that character. For this reason, there are moral obligations in justice against the manufacture, distribution, and sale of pornography, for example. Moreover, although the primary agents of public morality, the ones with the foremost responsibility for inculcating virtue, are families, churches, and institutions of civic society, law and government play a crucial though subsidiary role in public morality by supporting these primary actors. At both these levels, errors arise from abdicating or overstepping responsibilities proper to the non-governmental or governmental instances. The major question that George addresses is how the "police powers" of government extend not only to the protection and advancement of health and safety, but also to the protection and advancement of public morals. He thus distinguishes the powers that state and federal governments have as general jurisdictions (state) or delegated and enumerated powers (federal). This erudite but clear explanation outlines the types of moral limitations imposed by "police powers," for example, concerning transportation of women across state lines for immoral purposes—prostitution—and the mailing of obscene materials. The nature of these police powers can best be understood with the help of a definition of public morality: "the moral uprightness of individual people and the associations they form, considered insofar as it is a public good." Thus, public morals legislation regulates the behavior of individuals, limiting their choices and behaviors, in order to protect the public good. Public morals laws regulate private conduct when it threatens to harm the public interest, traditionally forbidding practices such as prostitution, adultery, and pornography. Common counterarguments to employing legislation and police powers in these areas either suppose that these behaviors are truly private when engaged in by consenting adults or distinguishes non-commercial sexual vice by appealing to "autonomy," "privacy," or "moral independence." In the heat of this debate, George and Dworkin agree, in one regard at least, that there are negative public consequences resulting from private acts. Specifically, they both identify pornography as having negative effects on those who use it and make it. However, despite its harm to the public interest, Dworkin argues that government should refrain from criminalizing pornography because individuals have a basic right to equal concern and respect, which grounds a right of moral independence. No one person's moral conception should outweigh another's. However, George adroitly indicates that persons who hold particular positions are not at stake in such laws, but rather the basis for law is found in the position itself and in the reasons and arguments that public morals legislation considers. Thus laws against pornography, prostitution, adultery, fornication, or drug abuse do not conflict with the right to equal concern and respect. At another level, George takes nuanced exception to John Finnis's position that the political common good is an instrumental human good, rather than an intrinsic and basic one. This distinction serves as a basis for Finnis's advocating the limitation of political authority to use coercion to promote virtue and repress vice, as such. This question parallels the non-retributive goals that punishment systems set in efforts at deterrence and rehabilitation. George argues for a benevolent form of moral paternalism, which does not exclude "in principle" laws against private behavior, such as fornication and adultery. However, in practice, George takes a similar tack (to that of Finnis and Thomas Aquinas) in saying that "there are often compelling prudential reasons for law to tolerate vices, lest efforts to eradicate them produce worse evils still."

In "The Maladies of the Political Class: When Reasons Cease to Matter," Hadley Arkes employs witty prose to address serious matters: moral injury, honor, honesty, counterfeit and true virtue, reliable evidence in moral matters, and moral reasons. He calls upon James Wilson, one of the American Founders, Montesquieu, Aristotle, Kant, Lincoln, and John Paul II, in the doing. With considerable insight into political philosophy, Arkes identifies the bases of law and morality found in the classic understanding of moral order (Aristotle) and the structure of moral judgments that flow from the idea of a rational creature as such (Kant). He argues (with the support of James Wilson) that a "local ethic" is inadequate for law. For if there were no higher appeal, what resistance could one give to character defamation, the misdeeds of the Third Reich, or the sexual misconduct of a president? Arkes illustrates the importance of the human search to know what is true based on knowledge of universal principles, and what is just based on understanding the rightful and wrongful ends of political life. This is particularly salient in the domain of public policy and constitutional law. Beyond the limitations of empiricists' approaches, legal positivism, or voluntarism, Wilson offers a fine example of grounding law and the Constitution in the principles of jurisprudence, "the philosophy of mind," and the nature of the human person. He thus offers a way to understand the possibility of consent to just law. Arkes addresses the question of interpreting the central truth of the Declaration of Independence on which the republic was founded: that "all men are created equal." Rather than treating each person in the same way (since differences prevail, for example, being innocent or guilty of a crime), this proposition means not only judging each person by the same standard, but also giving reasons for laws and judgments in order to be able to elicit obedience and consent. To deny the rational nature of moral truths and the possibility of understanding reasons concerning matters of right and wrong undercuts the ground of natural or human rights and government by consent. Neither the relativism of moral truth (suggested by Darwinians), nor the modern historian's agnostic stance to moral truth claims (Carl Becker), nor mere belief in the moral plausibility of a cause (as in the case of terrorists), nor the simple description of a gross behavioral act (adultery), nor the external appearances and circumstances of acts (killing a fetus inside, instead of outside, the womb), will satisfy the conditions needed for human moral agency. Before casting a moral judgment we need to understand the nature of the act and the intention animating the actor. Before consenting to government, persons need to understand the reasons for laws as well. Beyond pragmatic or utilitarian approaches, such as those proposed by Judge Richard Posner, Arkes argues for an approach based on the exercise of prudence, that is, the employment of moral principles with practical wisdom. Acting in a principled manner renders society more stable, since people are better off, by and large, when principles are known and respected, and when a justification is given for departing from customary applications of principles (that is, in appeals to higher principles). Natural rights are the basis for the possibility of understanding the human person and what is right or wrong in practical action. There is need for moral argument about the rational bases of law in the public forum in order to manifest the moral substance of the political system itself. Arkes makes an appeal to the necessity of providing such reasons and the training of the political class in this art.

In order to understand the radical challenges made to these philosophical, ethical, and legal considerations, we need to consider contemporary conceptions of the human person. Psychology has strongly influenced current understandings of the self, its development and health, and even the possibility of being moral or responsible. In his essay, "From the Modern Individual to the Transmodern Person," Paul C. Vitz gives an overview of modern and postmodern psychological notions of the self and the individual, in order to present a renewed, transmodern understanding of the person. Modern theories of the self have made marked contributions to contemporary psychology: for example, Sigmund Freud and the psychoanalytic tradition concerning human conscious, unconscious, and ego strength; and Carl Jung concerning self-actualization, individuation, and integration of unconscious universal archetypes. Likewise, Carl Rogers and Abraham Maslow have contributed their ideas on self-realization and self-development, which in popular culture, though, have sometimes taken narcissistic turns. Postmodern critiques of modern theories of the self and the individual have identified two problems in modern views. First, modern psychology has failed to ground the self in a cogent rationale. Second, postmodern thinkers have established a critique of the self, which they conceive of as a social construct dependant on historically determined phenomena. For their own part, postmodern theories, according to Vitz's analysis, have expressed a type of death wish, further deconstructing the self, which they see as diffuse (Kenneth Gergen), illusory (Philip Cushman), or non-existent (Robert Landy). Vitz argues that the postmodern critique of modernism has prepared the ground for a next step, which is felicitous for Judeo-Christian thinkers and psychologists. The "transmodern person" presents an alternative, transforming the modern understanding of the person and transcending it. Vitz thus courageously offers a definition of the person and the self with religious, social, and cosmic dimensions. He offers theological reflections (drawing upon Ashley, Torrance, and Ratzinger) and psychological theories that give priority to relationship, developed in a social context and lived out in love (compare the double commandment to love God and neighbor). He emphasizes the corporeal aspect of the human person, employing neurobiological and linguistic sciences. Moreover, suggesting a metaphysical grounding for the person, he highlights the process of becoming a relational person, open to intimacy, self-disclosure, friendship, and a sustained moral life.

After these ethical, political, and psychological considerations comes a more explicit treatment of religion and its importance for the person and the democratic polis. In the essay "The First Institution of Democracy: Tocqueville on Religion: What Faith Adds to Reason," Michael Novak treats one of the great modern social thinkers, Alexis de Tocqueville, concerning the relevance of religion to a modern democratic republic. During his visit to early-nineteenth-century America, Tocqueville discovered a vibrant society and a form of democratic order that expressed several original qualities: voluntary organizations, the democratic individual, equality in practice, liberty, enlightened self-interest, and so on. For example, Tocqueville saw in the voluntary associations that pervaded daily American life a form of self-government and a first law of democracy. However, he feared that the American lust for equality would push democrats to a tyrannical form of government that would tend to swell to provide every service and remove every difficulty—a "soft despotism." He thus predicted the clash between liberty and equality that is found in the welfare state of social democracy. Concerning "self-interest rightly understood," he observed that enlightened love of self constantly brought these Americans to aid each other and the state, performing daily deeds that serve the common good, although describing them as done in the interest of oneself and one's family. Tocqueville made two surprising claims: (1) that religion is the first political institution of the American democracy, and (2) that one day Catholics might well have a particularly advantageous footing for defending the presuppositions of democracy. Both of these claims challenge secularized writers who see the opposite to be the trend or the future of America. However, the Judeo-Christian tradition conceives of the human person in terms of three biblical principles that contribute to the hardiness of democratic institutions: personal dignity in freedom, equality in God's sight, and the immortal value of each person. Moreover, this religious tradition has supplied other benefits to democracy in America, as so many strengths that faith adds to reason. First, faith rectifies morals and behavior, as was shown by the enterprising Americans who drew moral principles from their religion. Second, biblical faith offers solid and durable ideas about God and human nature that influence conduct: ideas like the unity of humankind, and duties to God and neighbor. Third, religion resists the materialist pressure that democracy seems to favor. Religion, especially belief in immortality, can check and correct the downward pull of the principle of equality, and can even encourage greatness. Fourth, faith motivates the pursuit of high standards, even in private. Fifth, religion helps to protect the marriage bond and shape the mores established in the home, providing a basis for trust in the public sphere as well. Strong domestic self-governance and virtue thus aid civil governance. Lastly, Tocqueville notes how the spirit of religion and the spirit of liberty work in harmony and lend each other support. Throughout this analysis, Novak displays a gift for articulating the implications of Tocqueville's Christian insights about how faith contributes to understanding truth, freedom, and dignity, which all serve as interdependent preconditions for democracy today.

With its synthetic appeal to theology and to key insights from the other authors, Romanus Cessario's contribution, "Moral Realism and Christian Values," serves as a capstone for the collection. His essay goes to the heart of the issue, "the First Thing," God, who communicates to the Church of Christ with infallible truthfulness all that is required for salvation. The Church in turn embodies this faith and proclaims values to the secular society. Since God bestows the "theologal" life within the communion of the Church, Christian moral realism accepts not only that "the moral dimension of life is an integral feature of how things are" (as Robinson affirms in his essay), but also that "how things are" is best discovered in the single Church of Christ, which subsists in the Catholic Church and its living tradition and Magisterium. Not restricted to simply establishing guidelines for ethical conduct, the Church offers a crown for moral realism that is found in the practice of religion, prayer, and the Christian virtues. The three vocations in the Church—the priesthood, the consecrated life, and the laity—mediate the theologal life through their patterns of reciprocal relationships; each of these patterns involves the perfection of human nature by divine grace. Motivated by the virtue of pastoral charity, the presbyterate stands in service to the others, mediating the dynamics of the theologal life and the Gospel, by preaching revealed truths of the moral life that give us the hope for the transformation of the affective life through moral virtue. Moreover, the priest, through the sacraments and prayer life of the Church, mediates an affective union between the person and Christ. The fraternity of consecrated persons witnesses to the theologal life as a form of inclusiveness rooted in the communion of the Church. It offers an alternative to modern individualism and forms the matrix for the flourishing of the transmodern person (as Vitz conceives). The witness of the evangelical counsels of poverty, chastity, and obedience offers a reminder of the radical nature of Christian conversion, faced with a culture of consumption, permissiveness, and a thirst for power. The laity, for their part, are called to live the theologal life in the world. Their work of evangelization is the heart of their office and personal identity, apart from any particular roles and tasks within the Church. In accord with the Second Vatican Council, Cessario affirms that the Eucharist is the sacrament of ecclesial unity, by which God gathers the laity, consecrated persons, priests, and bishops together in Christ's love in order to give them strength as His instruments to sanctify the world according to the vocation of each. These three circles of ecclesial communion, as members of the Mystical Body of Christ, work to win the world back for moral realism. Cessario concludes that this moral realism finds in Jesus Christ and the celebration of the Eucharist the source for living the gifts of grace in the Christian virtues and for confidence to evangelize the world.

Beyond the limitations that are inherent in the human condition, such an integrated vision of the human person and the democratic polis as found in the following essays opens the door to hope for the future—the future of each person and nation in the context of the future that God holds in His hands. Even if it is guaranteed that no one will find his or her beatitude or complete happiness in any human relationship or community, a Christian realist vision provides the basis for making sense of each person's quest for goodness and truth, for loving family relationships, and for stable human institutions, even when they are in some way troubled, incomplete, or in development. The driving force behind the human spirit will continue to encourage us to better the world, without the utopian illusion that technical progress can assure human fulfillment. Intelligent dialogues between the sciences, philosophy, and religion (like those found here following)—about human dignity and beatitude, moral responsibility and values, law and custom, community and institutions—contribute potent means for nourishing the person and constructing the polis with the insights of reason strengthened by the surety of faith or Christian intelligence.

one

Kenneth L. Schmitz

A CONTEMPORARY PHILOSOPHY

OF ACTION

ACTION, in its highest form, is individual and personal. And so in taking up the topic of a contemporary philosophy of action, I will put before you the figure of an individual, an "acting person" around whom I will center my thoughts. He is a person who has acted out his ideas and values in a dramatic way; not as the CEO of a multinational corporation, nor the general of armies, nor the president of a republic, yet he has moved others to action. There can be no doubt that he has made his mark on the world stage. I refer to Karol Wojtyła, Pope John Paul II.

What is remarkable about the life of John Paul is not only that he brought together in his personality and career a contemporary form of action that has caught the spirit of the times and the attention even of those who dissent from his defense of several countercultural values, a defense that goes against the present grain of much opinion.

What is perhaps more significant is that, not only has he brought together in his personality and career a contemporary form of action, he has written about just such action. Moreover, with characteristic single-mindedness, he has lived out his own prescription for a contemporary "philosophy of action." It is rare that one finds an artist who can write clearly about what it is to be an artist; and even rarer to find a man of action who can explore with us the basic structure of human action. John Paul has been a kind of lightning rod in the latter part of the last century and the first years of this one, for the expression of human as well as spiritual and religious values—a rod that has attracted to itself the very forces and modalities that are emerging in the contemporary form that action is taking today.

Action not motion

First of all, however, we need to clarify the use of terms in the present situation; for everyday life and language with its practical demands leaves little room and has little need for precision in terms. It presses us with other things to do, important things. Clarification is needed, however, when we try to understand what we have been doing.

There is a body of philosophical analysis—which you may not have felt the need to consult before charging off to the office or school or elsewhere—that says there is a difference, and a great deal of difference, between motion and action. Indeed, they are in opposite corners of the ring, like before and after, early and late, warm and cold, passive and active. Of course, in the real world, action and motion are bedfellows, and are mixed together in actual human events. We distinguish them in thought, however, so that they may be directed back into that world for a better understanding of it and of ourselves.

Consider a relatively new Olympic sport, luge. As the sled slides down the run, we are compelled to watch as though watching paint dry at high speed; that's motion. But the winner has not fallen into first place, he has driven there, with—as far as I know—a mechanism as small as a dinosaur's brain. Of course, it is the slightly larger human brain, embedded in the person, that has played a part in managing the process. And so we have our distinction. Motion is "being moved by another," whether that is being blown off course by the wind, being baked by the sun, or being let down slopes by the law of gravity.

Action, on the other hand, is what we do; or rather, not just we. For a spark in the ignition explodes in the cylinder, once it is moved to act: here we have physical action. Among living things, a tree root reaches out to suck in the nutrients of its environment as its branches lift its leaves toward rain and shine: here we have vital action; and here too we discern an internal principle of development, a life force or living soul or however we designate it. Still, wherever we find action in this world we find motion mixed in with it. The wolf is moved by its prey, and we mostly by our bodily and felt needs.

But the example of the wolf introduces something new into the combination of motion and action. For the wolf is moved by what he sees, hears, or smells, and by what he remembers and has experienced; for he is a knower and acts out of his knowledge. It is a knowledge that is closely tied to his immediate environment and his sensory awareness of it: here we have conscious action. This is a new factor in action: the knowledge factor, and we need to pay attention to it, if we are to understand human action.

Once one considers the human agent—and by this term I do not mean someone who sells insurance or real estate, but the initiator of a course of action—once a human person considers doing something, a special form of awareness or knowledge—species-specific—comes into play from the beginning and persists throughout. Human action, however, is not simply and exclusively thought-engendered activity, since it is not the mind that acts but the whole person. And so, human action is situated within a complex organization in which many forces in addition to intelligence are at work.

Once one considers what is operative in human action, several forms of awareness come into play, including our sensory perceptions, feelings, and intelligence. A sense of awareness impregnates the field of human action. We are no longer dealing with a mechanical-chemical explosion in the cylinder of a machine, nor the outreach of a tree, nor even the hunt of the wolf. Rather, a complex awareness provides the final motive and the formal means of human action, and produces distinctive results that leave their trace both upon the one who acts and the world about him or her.

A new accent

Now, the preferred forms of action change as human society changes. I mean that there is a sort of fashion in the preferred types of action. When we look at the recent kinds of human action, we see a shift in the emphasis and value given to certain seemingly preferred forms of action; the basic structure of this species-specific activity remains, but it is given a new accent. One has only to visit a museum of industry and technology to be carried back a century or more to the great mechanical monsters, mostly steam-driven, that were the instruments of the men who drove them to produce great bulky products. The model of action in industrial society was manufacturing, and heavy manufacturing at that.

It is characteristic, however, of technology that it progresses in a way that other aspects of human life, such as morals or religion or poetry, do not. For technology values efficiency, economy of action. I can remember the early photocopy machines in the institute where I was a graduate student in the late '40s and early '50s. They filled a good part of a small room, and labored to produce a relatively meager result. Still, it was an improvement over typing and re-re-typing manuscript pages or staining your fingers with the ink of a mimeograph machine.

Or again, on my grandfather's farm in Canada during the '30s, the capability of plowing a field increased exponentially over the short period of a decade, from 5 acres in one day to 25 acres and then to 125 acres in the same period of time. The social effect of this was to reduce the number of workers who had to be employed in the field of agriculture, and in most industrially developed countries it has dropped below 3 percent of the work force, while increasing the agricultural yield at the same time. This reduction has led to a redistribution of the kinds of work performed in such societies as ours.

I am not aware that anything quite so dramatic has happened in industrial society, but something comparable to it has taken place in what has been called the "post-industrial" economy. The paradigm of what it means to act has moved away from emphasis upon the production of external goods, without, of course, denying the continuing and basic necessity of such production. It is just that more and more of the population finds itself in what is called "the service sector." Labor unions, at first engaged in the heavy manufacturing industries, such as mining and steel, have not found it easy to retain their prominence and influence in the shift to so-called "white-collar" service jobs. And this development has been accelerated by the revolution in telecommunication, the transmission of information (and alas! of misinformation) as a prominent type of action.

Emphasis upon an external product to be produced has shifted to a less tangible objective and has directed itself toward persons to be served in some fashion, by information, advice, guidance, care, or entertainment. Nor are we speaking here about relatively simple work, such as office cleaning, but also of services that require a highly skilled and expert knowledge. And it is these jobs that, for the most part, bring the highest economic rewards. Since the activity does not consist in relatively repetitive assembly work, but attention to clients' wishes, a successful discharge of service needs to be animated with certain personal characteristics—even to mimicking personal attention by substituting such service with answering machines and the like in sustaining the drive for efficiency.

This shift in the prominence of a certain kind of activity characterized by "service to others" has prepared for a fresh reflection on the nature of activity. It is here that, before he became pope, Karol Wojtyła had already laid the grounds for an understanding of human activity that "fits" the present trend and accounts in some measure for the audience he gained—even among non-Catholics and among dissenting Catholics—as an effective presence in the world arena. But before we take up his own "philosophy of action," it will be helpful to consider the circumstances and influences that shaped his personality and came to expression in his thought and career.

First element: culture

It is not incidental that he was a child of Poland, deeply encultured in its language, poetry, and theater. For this remarkable nation in Middle Europe was surrounded throughout most of the past two centuries by three great powers only too willing to deny that nation its existence: Germany, Austro-Hungary, and Russia. Stripped of its political institutions, it retained its memory, its language, and its culture. It was this heritage that drew the young Karol Wojtyła to the study of its resources.

Later this central focus on culture, born of necessity and suffering, suggested to the young adult Karol a new approach to the massive modern dilemma of collectivism and individualism as a problem of action. The lines between state collectivist programs and private individual initiatives, between socialism and capitalism, had been drawn and redrawn ad nauseam; the arguments had been rehearsed, been heard, been accepted or rejected by the same parties, so that nothing changed.

The field on which Wojtyła chose to do battle as a young student, and later as professor, pastor, and bishop, was not that of the politics of state collectivism and its opponent individual liberalism, but the undercurrents of culture that sustained and inspired a people in their everyday life as well as in their aspirations. This new ground of action

was unfamiliar to the Communist governors and to the advantage of
Wojtyła. It was as though he made an end run around and behind
a well-established political front line. It was to the sense of dignity
and pride in the Polish people and their culture to which Wojtyła ap-
pealed as he worked through what was to become his "philosophy of
the acting person."

To put this in social and political terms: instead of individualism
and collectivism, Wojtyła—drawing upon the Catholic heritage that
sustained the people in the days of their oppression—drew upon a
new relation, that between person and community. Nor was this simply a narrow rhetorical trick. On the contrary, it broadened the scope
of the issue of action to take account—not simply or principally of the
heavy industrial five-year plans—but of the rich texture of human life,
including art and religion. So that the artist and writer, as much as the
producer, could contribute to the life of the nation.

The turn to culture, then, represents the initial contribution, the
first element of what was to become Karol Wojtyła's philosophy of action. It is well known that he has written five extant dramas, rooted
in the religious history of the West and in the poetic literature of the
Polish nation. He has also written poems, some reflecting his industrial work experience at the Solvay chemical factory. It is known, too,
that he was engaged in the production and performance of the un-
derground theater that came to be known as the "theater of the living word."

Here to "act" in the theatrical sense of portraying a dramatic character merged with a political act of defiance against the occupying
Nazi regime and its successor. This protest acted out in the face of
considerable danger was a deliberate act of freedom. It is worth notic-
ing, however, that serious as his opposition was to those who were de
facto in power, he did not turn against the principle of legitimate authority, but made a distinction between authority and tyranny.

Second element: prayer life and spirituality

No doubt, this cultural resistance was grist for Wojtyła as he began to elaborate his own understanding of human action. But a second spiritual element came to him through his Catholic roots, and in particular through his intense prayer life, inherited in part from his father. This was enhanced by his early devotion to the Rosary. For it was in meeting the mystical tailor Jan Tyranowski in his years as a student in Krakow, and his association with the "Circle of the Living Rosary," that he developed a profound sense of the interior reality of his own and others' lives.

That prayer life found intellectual articulation in his first dissertation at the Angelicum University in Rome, where he wrote a thesis on the doctrine of faith in the writings of the Carmelite mystic St. John of the Cross. His devotion to an interior prayer life focusing upon the Rosary is evident in the papal encyclicals, which end invariably with praise and supplication to Mary. One of them closes with the invitation: Come let us philosophize at the table of Mary. So far, then, we have two preparatory ingredients in his reflections on human action: culture and prayer.

Third element: the classical structure of action

Before Karol Wojtyła, as John Paul II, became an actor on the world stage, he had gained a reputation as a philosopher who analyzed the notion of human action and wrote of it in his philosophical publications. When he was working in the Solvay chemical factory during the occupation of Krakow by the Nazis, he found time in his recurrent rest periods to read from a scholastic textbook on metaphysics. The experience was world-revealing for him. Up until then he had been a student of philology and literature, and had not dreamed about a region of thought that sought to get at the very roots of things.

It was not until more than a dozen years later, however, during his second year as a young teacher of philosophical ethics at the free University of Lublin in 1955, that he was able to develop an outline of the roots of human action. He didn't start his thought-project from nowhere, however, but methodically gathered up the classical elements of a philosophy of action. He did this by canvassing the history of philosophy from Plato to Jeremy Bentham and the modern utilitarians, in order to see what other philosophers in the past had said about human action. And he found there in the classical and traditional sources much of substance for his own philosophical thought. In this way, he established continuity with the past, "remaining [as he put it] in the area of the philosophy of existence."[1]

From Plato he took the primacy of the Good—the conviction that properly human action is motivated by a desire for the good (even if we sometimes mistake what is really good). From Aristotle he took the principle of development, as we grow from the potential with which we begin in our mother's womb and arms to what we might actually become in our mature years. From Augustine he learned that the Good was not simply a transcendent Form but a personal reality who calls upon us to participate in its own divine goodness in and through acts of love. From Thomas Aquinas he discovered the root of all being in the supreme principle of existential actuality, of our fundamental presence among the community of beings; he acknowledged at the heart of each and every thing the energy that sustains it above the encroaching shades of non-existence and that permeates each being with the energy of actual existential presence.

With these notions in mind, the young philosopher composed a metaphysical pattern of action whose traditional structure was later to be transformed in the encounter with modern philosophy. But already he thought himself able to show the shortcomings of the merely

---

1. Adam Boniecki, *The Making of the Pope of the Millennium: Kalendarium of the Life of Karol Wojtyła*, trans. Irena and Thaddeus Mirecki (Stockbridge, Mass.: Marian Press, 2000), p. 383.

utilitarian and narrowly functional morality that is so prevalent in to-day's society, and to shape his own broader and deeper understanding of human action.

So far, then, we have the elements of culture, prayer, and conti-nuity with the classical human past; but now we turn with him to the need to engage modernity with its new insights and demands.

Fourth element: modern consciousness

Owing much to the great classical thinkers, nevertheless he did not find himself shut up in that world. He had experienced too much of the great century of suffering and of brutal action against all that is precious in humanity—the forced movement of peoples unprecedent-ed since the barbarian invasions of 1,500 years ago, genocide on a new scale, but also exceptional courage in the face of tyranny. Upon his re-turn from Rome with a doctorate in theology, and after a brief period of welcome pastoral work, he was put under obedience to complete a second doctorate, this time in philosophy.

At this point, broader forces in the intellectual field of Europe came to his notice. Most notable among them was the movement of phenomenology. Now this revolution in philosophical thought had occurred at the beginning of the twentieth century under the lead-ership of the German Jewish philosopher Edmund Husserl. An ac-complished philosopher of mathematics, he challenged the current mechanistic view that turned the inner life celebrated by the poet and novelist into a toolbox of mental nuts and bolts, as though the human person were a wired machine. Instead Husserl's phenomenology redi-rected learned attention to the reality of "lived experience." This turn to the human subject was not simply to an objective pattern of behav-ior, caught up in a network of external connections, nor even simply one being enmeshed among others, but rather a turn to a very special kind of being, at whose center is a distinctive mental life. Phenome-nology provided a method for exploring the various activities of our conscious life, and engaged human subjectivity and personal interiority in the world of lived experience and concrete action. This had the effect of opening up doors to evidence and experience from which the mechanistic method remained closed; so that one could explore the contours, not only of the mechanistic movements of the brain, but artistic and poetic activity, religious experience, and the rich variety of emotional experience that are part of everyone' s everyday life. Phenomenology now made all that accessible by a trustworthy method of analysis.

After the faculty of theology in the Jagiellonian University in Krakow was shut down by the Communist authorities, Wojtyła received an appointment as professor of ethics in the newly reorganized Catholic University of Lublin, which proudly boasted of being the only free university between the Baltic and the Pacific. In his first year of teaching (1954–55), not surprisingly, after the manner of most newly graduated teachers, he presented the problem of action more or less as he had developed it in his dissertation. He sought to sail between Scylla and Charybdis. Scylla was the philosopher Immanuel Kant, who had so purified moral action that it was treated as the exclusive activity of a pure reason, utterly disdainful of and divorced from any feelings, emotions, or desires that might arise from our sensory appetites and our bodily mode of being. It was a pure rational ethics of duty.

Now Wojtyła had no aversion to duty, and he admired Kant's defense of the human person as having a value that could never be subordinated to merely utilitarian aims. For Wojtyła agreed with Kant that the person must always be respected as having a dignity in and of itself. But the price Kant had paid was to divide the human individual in half, leaving aside the entire dimension of his bodily existence, and relegating all such activity to mere utility, something less than fully human.

The second philosopher, as counterpoint to Kant, was another German, the phenomenologist Max Scheler, who protested against the pure formalism of such an understanding of human action, and who restored the understanding of human life to its fuller context as the experience of a wide range of values—including values of utility, but also higher values of beauty, friendship, love, and the sacred, each of them fraught with emotion. Wojtyła was inspired by such a rich context for human action; but, if Kant was his Scylla, then Scheler was his Charybdis, for he found Scheler too passive in the mere experience of values, too little concerned with the demands of action. To Wojtyła's mind, what counted was the role of the will and the decision to act, based upon knowledge that was worthy of properly human action. Fortified by the classical elements of a theory of action and now forearmed with a contemporary method of analysis, the philosopher of Krakow laid out his own reflections on the kind of action that could be effective in the contemporary situation.

His mature thought

It is well known that mathematical geniuses flourish early and then settle down to more ordinary activity; philosophers, on the other hand, usually take a while longer and then go on and on and on. Karol Wojtyła was in his late forties and had been a bishop for almost a dozen years, archbishop for almost half a dozen, and cardinal for two, when he completed his mature philosophy of action with the publication of the work that became known in the English-speaking world as *The Acting Person.*[2]

The year of publication, 1969, had been a busy one, integrating thought and action. It included scores of parish visitations, archdiocesan meetings, regional liturgies, and lectures throughout Poland, including a lively participation in the philosophical and theological life of the nation. There were pastoral visits to the sick of the diocese, "house by house," twenty houses in two days on one occasion, many meetings with religious and lay, with married couples, children, youth

2. Karol Wojtyła, *The Acting Person,* trans. Andrzej Potocki (Dordrecht and Boston: D. Reidel Publishing Company, 1979; original in Polish: *Osoba i Czyn,* 1969).

and students, a visit to two synagogues to strengthen Jewish-Catholic understanding, initiatives for implementing the reforms of the Second Vatican Council in the diocese (a program which was carried to completion over a ten-year period), suggestions for a new catechism (which he spoke of as taking a "totally new approach"), and the establishment of an Institute of Family Studies.

Beyond the borders, he had gone to Vienna and Rome, for participation in a symposium for Dialogue with Unbelievers, with the Council of the Laity, and participation in the international synod of bishops in Rome. He had also undertaken a month-long visit to Canada and the United States. His book *The Acting Person* had appeared in December of that year, and a few weeks later, at Christmas, as he had done for the past ten years, he celebrated midnight mass "in the open fields at Nowa Huta" just outside Krakow.[3] This city of steel mills—of the "new ovens"—had been planned by the Communist masters as a "city without God." By constant pressure and resistance despite obstacles put in the way, however, construction of the Church of the Ark had begun two years previously, in 1967.

Earlier in the year 1969, while dedicating the stone which had come from the Church of Constantine in Rome, and which was to become the cornerstone of the new great Ark Church in Nowa Huta,[4] the cardinal had said to the assembled faithful: "We Christians, we who profess Christ, who want to create the presence of God by erecting a temple for Him, we also want to create things of this world. [Here is the call to action; he continues:] It is not true, my dear brothers and sisters, [as government propaganda had charged] that we do not want to create the things of this world. Or that the Church will hinder us in doing that! The Church is an inspiration for us, an inspiration to create a new world! To create Nowa Huta!"

During the writing of the book on action, it was the author's hab-

3. George Weigel, *Witness to Hope: The Biography of Pope John Paul II* (New York: Cliff Street Books, 1999), p. 180.

4. Boniecki, *The Making of the Pope*, p. 364.

it to work in the mornings seated before the altar in the cathedral church of the Wawel in Krakow, the ancient church redolent with the mysteries of Christ and the cultural memories of the nation. We read in the opening pages that "man must not lose sight of his proper place in the world which he himself has shaped—and that is the world of culture and civilization, i.e. the 'contemporary world' that we [here he refers to the bishops assembled during the Second Vatican Council] considered with such care while preparing the constitution *Gaudium et Spes* [*The Church in the Modern World*]."[5]

As he developed his mature analysis of human action, drawing on an earlier book with its frank discussion of human sexuality and love, the first major distinction he drew was between what merely happens to us and what we actively do. What "merely happens" to us either comes to us from outside, from other persons, or from things, or happens within the movement of our bodily processes over which we have little direct control, and of which we are normally not conscious. It is usually only when we have a headache or indigestion or are not feeling well that these physiological processes manifest themselves in our conscious life. At most, they provide a kind of background body-tone to the rest of our existence. They are best left to the special sciences and to a healthy daily regimen. Nonetheless, we can discern here, as well as in his mountain hiking, skiing, and kayaking, the later development of his "theology of the body."

But if our bodily processes remain, for the most part, below the threshold of consciousness, it is quite other with our emotional life. For we are directly and sometimes vividly conscious of our feelings, which register an unstated and non-verbal relationship with the world outside us as well as the lived world within. A part of that world within is the subconscious, which is the dimension of our personality that both suppresses destructive movements of our psyche (as Freud has told us so insistently) but also that more positively nourishes our creativity. So much, then, for what "happens" to us.

---

5. Boniecki, *The Making of the Pope*, p. 383.

We come at last to what is unique to human action. Action that is properly and distinctively and exclusively human is performed with deliberate thought and free decision, so that the human quality of our actions passes through both knowledge and liberty. Not every action, not everything we enact, is distinctively human. From his earlier study, Wojtyła accepts the classical distinction between acts that are performed by human beings as well as by other animals but that are not exclusive to humans, acts such as breathing, digesting, sensing, and reacting; and he distinguishes these acts from those actions that possess the specifically human quality that is found in human action alone. Without this quality, there may be motion, or process, or emotion, and even a sort of action; but to the degree that we participate in the quality of humanity, actions must be thoughtful and uncoerced. And so a properly human act is not simply one that happens to be performed by a human being *(actus hominis)*, but one that participates in the distinctive quality of being human *(actus humanus)*, for we will find that quality nowhere except in ourselves.

And so to discover our humanity, we must enter within ourselves, to undertake a journey of self-discovery. In taking this turn to the subjective center, Wojtyła incorporates the introspective tendencies prevalent in modern culture, as he engages the modern concentration upon human consciousness. For that introspective tendency plays itself out in our contemporary fascination with psychology, and expresses itself in the modern novel, music, and the other arts. We have here, then, with the philosopher of Krakow, not only someone immersed in the ancient lore of the Church, but also one who has been nurtured by the events, the thought, and the creativity of the twentieth century. Moreover, he has combined the ancient background and the present introspective interest in order to articulate the contemporary meaning and nature of human action.

Let us begin the philosophical journey within ourselves. It begins with our conscious awareness of ourselves in the surrounding world. All sorts of signals are constantly coming into us. Many of them fall by the wayside for lack of attention on our part; indeed, we would be overwhelmed by information overload were it not for the spirit of abstraction that is indigenous to human nature, the ability to select and consider. The burgeoning information explosion, whether made explicit through telecommunication or left fallow and implicit as background noise, is part of the modern matrix with which the acting person must deal. Contemporary wisdom consists in knowing what to do with it all. Without the selectivity we would be overwhelmed. We attend to a few of the indicators, for one or another reason, because of our background or expectation, and to satisfy a need, or out of curiosity, or to shape our own self-image. And these select few fall within the sweep of our mind.

But now something rather remarkable happens. Wojtyła puts it this way: in turning our mind toward certain phenomena we place them in what he calls "the field of our consciousness." I suppose we might say that they are *available* to our attention, though we have not yet really attended to them. No doubt, you have had the experience of reading something, to find at the end of the page that you have assimilated all of the words but not really paid attention to their meaning, so that you need to retrace ground already passed over. If someone asks you: "Have you read the page?" you reply, somewhat hesitatingly, "Well, yes." But if you are further asked what it means, you have to admit that you will have to read it over again to find out.

It is only when you attend, are *actually present to,* the words already in the field of your consciousness that you appropriate them, that you make them your own by giving them your own mental mode of being; which is the mode of "understanding," the mode of "being attentive." Through our attention we make them part of the manifold of our experience, so that they may grow in us as seeds on the path of self-formation. They provide the germ, but we provide the soil of our response that determines their effect upon us, whether it be acceptance, rejection, or modification. Now they are really ours, and so they can play a role in shaping our character, molding who we are. In this *appropriation* we give to the mental events our own mode of being; they become part of us, of our experience and memory, and they contribute to our expectation.

Still, we have not yet reached the center of our inner journey of self-discovery. And we reach it only when we arrive at the consciousness of ourselves as capable of originating new lines of causality for which we are responsible. We come to know who we are when we uncover the freedom that lies at our core, and which is the source of our response. In this sense, we come closest to God in imaging his own creative freedom; and this is why, in what can only be called a genuine development of Church doctrine, already anticipated by the Second Vatican Council but made part of Church teaching through his encyclicals, John Paul has insisted that religious freedom, along with other freedoms, is an essential right pertaining to all human beings. In so doing and with all due corrections, he has adopted the modern language of human rights.

Now that we have arrived at the distinctive center of the human agent, the odyssey of self-discovery does not stop there at the source of action, anymore than a river stops at its headwaters. Rather, our freedom proceeds to become an odyssey of self-formation, of self-definition. For the inward development takes an outer turn as the action forms within us. In playing out our freedom, we deliberate on a course of action, consider it, choose it, and act upon that choice, so that the decision passes beyond us into the world, out beyond our reach: "What is done is done." This marks the dramatic quality of action; it leads us to make a difference, whether great or small, in the world, upon things and persons about us.

But our action does not come to rest there outside us. Instead, it returns to us, homing in on us and altering what and who we are, because of what we have done. This is the "shaping" that John Paul wrote of in the early pages of *The Acting Person,* and spoke of in his homily as he laid the corner stone of Nowa Huta. The recursive action both enters the world and re-enters us. Every action, in particular the major ones, comes home to us. We all experience this as we learn how to do things through doing. What was initially a clumsy effort becomes a skillful habitual activity. We need think only of the repetitive drills of the Olympic figure skaters, or ourselves as we learned to drive or read or write through familiar repetition. Yet, because of the spirit of abstraction, I can consider the acquisition of a technique without reference to the full human context of the operation.

But there is one kind of action, or rather an aspect of our activity, that does more than enhance our skill and ability to perform. This dimension of action determines our quality as persons, and we call that aspect of action "morality or ethics," the use or abuse of our human freedom. There is a certain moral quality that attaches to properly human actions: when we are acting distinctively as human, as only we among all things can act, we are drawn into the wide and deep circle of the good—to profit from it or misappropriate it. For the action passes, not only through the knowledge of things, but through their value as well.

This personal enhancement is not true of the merely technical aspects of our actions. If I consider a technical action abstractly, that is, without reference to the full human context in which the action plays itself out, I do not consider the recursive effect of the action upon my total quality as a person who has initiated it. I am oriented only on its successful performance. This means that I may play the piano well, but—in itself—that does not make me a good person as a whole; indeed, I may play it badly, and yet be a good person. If, however, I have talent and yet play it badly because I permitted my parents to sacrifice in order to pay for my lessons, but "goofed off" and did not practice, then—however slight the default in this rather petty case—my action was not a good one, and has done me no credit as a person. It is the moral weight of our actions that develops us as persons. And this is rooted in the native freedom that we possess and the obligation it brings with it. The recent hearings on Enron confirm this quality in each of us.

There is, then, a mysterious way in which, through our actions, we are linked to the possibility of the good that is meant to perfect us, and that will perfect us, if we but conform our freedom to and participate in that mysterious power. This is the ontological basis of natural law, the ethical law of human nature. Such law is more than a set of rules imposed from outside; it is a life-giving power. It is not only normative for us, guiding us in what we should do, but is perfective of us as to what and who we are.

Now this means that a properly human act is not simply an outer performance, a behavior; it means rather that such action has an inner life as well. It means, too, that each act has reciprocal relationships, both with the effect on others and with the agent him- or herself. And so we live in a dramatic situation, in which we increase or decrease the human value of our persons in and through our actions. This is what it means to live at the center of the human drama.

What this comes to, then, is this: that it is the internal quality of our actions that determines their human weight and their value. What gives them value is, first of all, the freedom that pulses at their center as we originate free lines of causality, shaping ourselves and the world about us. It is a freedom that is not simply an arbitrary impulse, but rather one that is meant to engage the reality of the situation, including the reality and the dignity of other persons with whom we live in community.

That is why John Paul has laid so much stress upon religious freedom, since that is freedom touching the deepest sector of our lives; but the emphasis is not only on religious freedom. In his social encyclicals, the value of freedom is everywhere. Thus, John Paul has stressed responsible entrepreneurship, the individual initiative of economic activity, so absent from the state collectivism experienced during his middle years and too easily abused by an irresponsible form of capitalism. The value of freedom is also why he has promoted and celebrated the work of artists, who image the very activity of the Creator. Here, as already mentioned, we have a development in Church teaching regarding the inner dynamic of human action.

One is called upon to engage in the reality of the contemporary situation, in the present world with neighbors, and to be responsible for the precious value of freedom, which is not to be misspent. Yet we are not without direction. For in that world and among our neighbors we find a compass for authentic action. That compass is the truth of things and others as they manifest their genuine value to us, so that action is meant to respond to the normative and perfective power of truth, to the way in which reality is in its deepest structure. We are free to pursue the truth about ourselves, others, and the world, and in that pursuit to bring about our maturity, and hopefully a betterment in the world. The task of building our character and influencing those around us to become more human is not an easy one. It calls for us to integrate the various facets of our complex being, our physical condition, our emotional life, our subconscious inclinations.

When we succeed we achieve a certain transcendence within ourselves as we cross an inner threshold in meeting a test and building a character. For each of the complex facets of the human person have their own immediate ends that, of themselves, do not easily fall into a harmonious unity. Instead, emotions may run amok, subconscious drives may imbalance us, fixed ideas may become obsessive; these and other factors mitigate against our freedom. It is only by struggling to submit to the truth as it manifests itself to us in concrete situations that we can realize the freedom which lies at the root of our distinctive way of being.

Of course, by no means everything we do throughout the day perfectly fulfills the demands of human action. There are distractions, and heavier still other factors: emotional blocks, conscious and subconscious, that seek to dominate our conduct and deprive it of its native freedom. Nevertheless, the possibility of genuinely free acts is not simply an empty and unfulfilled ideal.

There are signs of generosity strewn along the paths of our lives— flowers or lights or salt, the metaphors spill out their goodness and elusively signal hope. Breaking through to freedom is part of the human drama, and is recognized not only in heroic acts (as those of the firemen on 9/11 going into the maelstrom as others were fleeing the terror), but also in the daily discharge of obligations done out of quiet love for the good of others.

In a more settled and traditional society, the communal forms, the customs, mores, and laws, bear the weight of prescribed action. In our largely secular contemporary society, it is rather the acting person who is called upon to invest the customs and laws with their human quality. The new accent on action discloses the need of an inner validation of human values. That, indeed, is the deepest and highest demand of democracy. All the types of action remain in play, but the new accent centers on the internal core of human agency, which the secular world—rightly, yet too lightly—cherishes as freedom.

For we have not been left adrift, in a sea of conflicting forces, but have been provided with a compass for action with our fellow persons. A kind of ontological compass has been built into us and our environs, whose lodestar is the law of human nature grounded in the depth-structure of the world and our humanity.

It is this self-shaping, community-building, world-affirming action to which we are called; and beyond that, to something more, something greater, something not quite conceivable—to nothing less than the universal call to holiness.

two

≋

Daniel N. Robinson

IN DEFENSE OF MORAL REALISM

T IS, perhaps, less surprising after September 11 to attend a lecture
setting out to offer a defense of moral realism.[1] There are some actions so wanton in their indifference to life and in their selection of
victims as to put on notice most versions of moral relativism. I say
most versions, for the dominant moral perspective of the past two
centuries has left ample room for widespread—even nearly universal—moral judgments, while grounding these in what are finally the
merely contingent facts of human sentiment and human values. The
perspective has many defenders, even many fathers, but surely its authoritative expression was provided by David Hume. Recall the subtitle of his *A Treatise of Human Nature: Being an attempt to introduce*

---

1. Portions of this address are taken from my book *Praise and Blame: Moral Realism and Its Applications* (Princeton, N.J.: Princeton University Press, 2002).

the experimental method of reasoning into moral subjects. The "experimental method," as the eighteenth century would understand the term, was the method of systematic observation; in this case, a systematic *introspective* examination of just what it is that is most reliably associated with moral ascriptions. Just what is it, in Hume's famous phrasing, that is "constantly conjoin'd" with moral judgments? Hume's answer is given most economically in *An Enquiry Concerning the Principles of Morals* (Sec. 1):

> The final sentence, it is probable, which pronounces characters and actions amiable or odious, praise-worthy or blameable; that which stamps on them the mark of honour or infamy, approbation or censure; that which renders morality an active principle and constitutes virtue our happiness and vice our misery; it is probable, I say, that this final sentence depends on some internal sense or feeling, which nature has made universal in the whole species.

Against this very line of philosophical speculation I wish to put before you an alternative; less a theory than an argument to the effect that the grounds on which Humean theories of morals depend are thin and shifting and surely no more secure than the foundations available to a realist theory or morality. Here, I can offer no more than a hurried sketch of the defense. Indeed, in promising a defense of moral realism, I really promise too much. That defense would require far more time and effort than are available now. I should say that the fuller case is presented in *Praise and Blame*. Rather, let me draw from that work an assessment of the stock criticisms advanced by those who reject moral realism. In this way I will be able to present perhaps "half a defense"; not the constructive arguments in support of moral realism, but some of the critical arguments against its opponents. These targets of my criticism, as should now be obvious, must be all varieties of moral *relativism,* including those probably favored now in this very room. But these very terms—*realism* and *relativism*—are heavily laden with quirky and provincial connotations. We must be careful here. Some defenders of moral realism are defending not the existence of actual moral entities or properties, but rather the prevalence of certain feelings or judgments that are in some vague sense "moral." On this account, what is real is the psychological state, not its content. The patient in Ward-C truly believes he is a unicorn. The psychological state of belief is taken to be real; the content of the belief, non-existent.

Moral relativism has appeared variously, but always has that signal feature by which it can be recognized. It is important to be clear on this point. To argue that the ultimate *grounding* of moral judgments is *relative* to any of the following is finally *not* to argue as a moral relativist: human tendencies, cultural values, contextual factors, historical forces, hereditary predispositions, sentiment. Rather, the moral relativist is one who contends not simply that moral judgments are thus grounded, but that their very *validity* is thereby and exhaustively established. I should draw the distinction in another way: in actual circumstances, it may well be that, for many, a correct moral appraisal arises as a result of what has been learned from the wider culture, or imposed by the present context, or closely tied to a personal feeling or sentiment made ever sharper as a result of certain biological processes. The moral realist may readily accept all this but then goes on to distinguish between *how* a right answer is reached in the matter of moral assessments and *what* the right answer is; or, more modestly, *that* there is a right answer, and one that is utterly independent of psychological, biological, and social contingencies. To say, then, that the target of criticism is moral relativism is to say that moral questions are questions about reality, and, as such, are subject to correct answers.

Against all this is the weight of current learned opinion which regards morality as inextricably bound up with the needs, habits, dispositions, and eccentricities of human nature, shaped by the shifting challenges and opportunities afforded by the environments in which that nature finds itself. Protean though that nature is, there is a strong genetic component so widely distributed as to create the appearance of moral absolutes. Behind the scenes, however, it is evolutionary pressure that has pruned and shaped the genome in such a way as to yield creatures with strong and common tendencies even under the widest range of cultural and local influences. The story thus told is coherent, the database broad and thick, and made even more compelling by the addition of those psychological processes of conditioning and acculturation that account for such variations as are evident in the anthropological literature.

I submit that there are good reasons to doubt the adequacy of this currently dominant view in all its variations. Consider first the standard Humean version: our moral judgments are based not on external realities but internal sentiments. Thus, the ontology of morals is not "out there" but within the emotional or affective framework of creatures of a certain kind. Hume was not alone in advancing such a theory; his is but the most influential among an entire school of moral *sentimentalists,* including Shaftesbury, Adam Smith, Hutcheson— the list is long.

This sentimentalist thesis continues to enjoy broad and devoted allegiance within philosophy, though, as I shall suggest, it is a strange thesis. We begin to see the theory's stress points when we acknowledge at the outset that persons making moral judgments understand themselves to be expressing something different from personal aversions, pleasures, or whims. There will be disagreement as to whether what is being affirmed is valid beyond the boundaries of their own culture or religious beliefs, but there will be widespread agreement that "good" and "evil," "right" and "wrong," "Well done!" and "Shame!" register something weightier than merely personal penchants.

The sheer peculiarity of sentimentalist theories of morality was put in still sharper focus by G. E. Moore. The question Moore raises is whether the reference of all moral or ethical ascriptions "is simply and solely . . . a certain feeling." If this were the case, Moore concludes, it would follow that "all the ideas with which Moral Philosophy is concerned are merely psychological ideas."[2] In addressing

2. G. E. Moore, "The Nature of Moral Philosophy," in *Philosophical Studies,* 1922.

the question, Moore finds, at least tentatively, that the sentimentalist thesis is opaque both as a moral psychology and as a philosophical doctrine. What troubled Moore can be instructively recast in the following way:

1. When I judge an action or event to be morally wrong I am judging it to be the sort of action or event that tends to excite within me feelings of, say, indignation.

2. When I judge one action or event to be clearly more wrongful than another, I am actually basing the judgment on my estimation of which would create a greater indignation were both to occur at the same time.

3. When *you* make the judgments given in (1) and (2), then you are estimating how the action or event would tend to excite feelings in *you*.

4. As neither of us has any means by which to know such tendencies in the other, there is simply no basis on which either of us can make sense of how the other is using words such as "wrong." Moral terms as such could not rise higher in their import than a kind of noise.

5. It follows then that between two such persons "there is absolutely no such thing as a difference of opinion on moral questions."[3]

The problem for the moral sentimentalist does not end here, for if the thesis is not about the relationship between moral judgments and the feelings of the particular judge, then about *whose?* Moore regards as simply implausible the view that moral judgments can be based on guesses as to how someone else might feel when facing an action or event of a certain kind. And it goes beyond implausibility to suppose that, in the given circumstance, one can estimate the feelings excited in "all mankind"! There is probably nothing in the realm of possible that would engender precisely the same sentiment in the entire hu-

---

3. See Robinson, *Praise and Blame,* ch. 1, n. 40.

man race. Nor is there any evidence to suggest that, in making moral appraisals, persons engage in some form of actuarial exercise to calculate the fraction or percent of the human community likely to be excited to levels of indignation by an action or event. This is all sufficient for Moore to conclude that, whatever the reference of moral terms, it is not merely a psychological state or idea.

The persistence of sentimentalism within the body of moral thought requires additional comment here, partly by way of rehearsal, partly by way of amplification. For better or for worse, it is an undeniable fact of psychological life that one's emotional reaction to wrongdoing is of a decidedly different character when one is the target rather than an uninvolved witness. The witness to historical events of a malevolent nature is able to condemn without sharing the actual feelings of those who were victimized. Nor would the estimation of wrongdoing be affected in any way at all were it proven that the victims—owing to treatment by drugs or surgery or hypnosis—did not mind what was being done to them. There are, it might be supposed, relatively few persons who feel the loss of a murdered child as acutely as do the parents, but the judgment that a terrible wrong has been committed is no less certain for that. To explain the judgment on the basis of "empathy" is to introduce all varieties of cognitive and conceptual resources well beyond the range of mere feelings. Sharing another's grief is at once to project oneself into the life of the other; to comprehend the other's scale of needs and values; to shadow the aspirations and imagine the memories by which the grief is deepened and uniquely personalized. Even when the assumptions of the moral sentimentalist are warranted, therefore, it is obvious that the part taken by sentiment *qua* sentiment is more as corollary than as cause. In a word, there is nothing at the level of psychology or of conceptual analysis capable of sustaining the main arguments of the moral sentimentalist.

I turn now to what might be called "behavioristic" conceptions of morality based on notions of reward and punishment. These, too, clearly miss the essential character of moral ascriptions as such as-criptions are actually deployed in the real world. Those who commit crimes are blamed, but those who do not are not praised! Moreover, to pay someone not to commit a violent crime would seem odd, and especially so as a form of "reward" or praise. It would be comparably peculiar to reward one for doing what everyone routinely does. Praise and blame are not reducible to material costs and penalties and are often blatantly out of place in the circumstance. Most would judge it to be insulting to offer a high salary to Mother Teresa, even on the assumption that this might encourage others to perform the saintly work for which she was known.

To the extent that they are at all akin to rewards and punishments, moral ascriptions are rewards and punishments of an unusual type. Consider one of the expected consequences of blame. When validly directed at a person, blame is expected to cause feelings of guilt, re-morse, and shame. When wrongly leveled it may often cause anger, indignation, even the impulse toward reprisal. For moral appraisals to achieve desired ends, at least four conditions must be met, each dif-ferent from those adequate to the purposes of ordinary rewards and punishments.

(A) First, the ascriptions must be *correct*. Heaping praise for hero-ism on the wrong person or blame for malfeasance on the innocent increases neither self-worth in the one nor shame in the other. Ac-cordingly, a straightforward behavioristic analysis of the efficacy of praise and blame inevitably leaves out too much, for neither "praise" nor "blame" can function as praise or blame unless it is apt.

(B) Furthermore, the praising and blaming of actions or events must match up with something relevant about the recipients and *ac-knowledged* as such by them. A cash prize given to the one-thousandth person entering the new supermarket is surely rewarding, but win-ning it is not laudatory. Increasing the rate of taxation of those with the highest earnings is a species of penalty, but not a condemnation. Again, the connotations of "praise" and "blame" are not fully paralleled by rewards and penalties. Nor are they simple performatives. When one says, "I promise," the utterance constitutes the actual performance. But when one says, "I praise," the utterance is subject to any number of tests and criteria having to do with the standing of the speaker, the aims and conduct of the intended beneficiary, the social and cultural values that qualify both the intentions, and the respective standing of speaker and target.

(C) Additionally, for praise or blame to be accepted as such, the source must be recognized as authoritative and not merely in possession of power or material resources. Not only must the dispensers of praise and blame have *standing*, but the standing must be relevant to the context. Praise for achievements in physics proffered by the coach of the winning football match would be no cause for pride. Indeed, in certain contexts, the character of the dispenser of blame could raise blame itself to the level of an honor while sinking praise to that of censure. Whether in the form of utterances or of palpable objects (statues, certificates, gold stars), praise and blame presume standing and authority on the part of the source. It is not the utterance or the object that carries the perceived moral content, but the office that bestows it, and the holder of that office.

(D) Finally, tied to these conditions is another: the efficacy and legitimacy of praise or blame depend upon *shared moral understandings* absent which the utterances and objects are unintelligible. It is owing to this feature that persons generally regarded as possessing utterly unique moral qualities—or frighteningly devoid of them—often and honestly wonder what all the fuss is about! I refer here to saints and psychopaths.

What some have concluded from this is that morality is but a species of consensus, formed within a given culture to satisfy the terms of life adopted by the members of that culture. Just in case, for whatever reason, one proves to be refractory in adhering to the local standards, one can expect to suffer the wages of sin. Praise and blame seem so fully dependent on context and on the shifting desiderata of majorities as to have no stable content at all. A personality that expresses itself in aggressive and hostile fashion may be little more than a genetic outcome and is thus not a question of vice or virtue but of luck, in this case *constitutive luck*. Whether these foreordained expressions of personality result in honor or incarceration is, on this theory, less a question of vice or virtue than of luck, in this case the *moral luck* of finding oneself in one culture rather than another or with one set of parents rather than another. At first blush, then, we seem to be steeped in sociological and psychological considerations that some would take as exhausting the sources and actual content of moral ascriptions.

This is not the end of the difficulty, for still unanswered are questions concerning *moral* standing and not simply "standing." I noted the requirement of a shared moral understanding, but what needs to be filled out is just what makes an understanding "moral," as well as the degree to which it must be shared for there to be a recognizable moral community. Tied to all this are enduring questions regarding the alleged subjectivity and relativity of morals, the allegedly unbreachable chasm between *is* and *ought,* and various perplexities nested within these. So, again, the moral realist faces serious and weighty challenges. Well, let us face them.

The apparent inadequacy of theories of moral realism and the supposed subjectivity of morals have been asserted in every age of sustained moral discourse, from remote antiquity to the present. Bernard Williams pointedly contrasts ethics and science in terms of the power of the latter to address questions that converge on ultimately settled answers. To explain the success of this convergence Williams attributes to scientific answers their representation of "how things are," whereas in ethics, ". . . there is no such coherent hope."[4] Indeed, whatever that calculus by which to gauge worthiness for praise or blame, it would seem to have little in common with the tried and true methods of science. Moral standards seems hopelessly internalized,

4. Bernard Williams, *Ethics and the Limits of Philosophy* (Cambridge, Mass.: Harvard University Press, 1985), p. 135.

even when constructed and maintained by the community. Indeed, "community standards" is a term referring only to those evaluative precepts that have been internalized by most if not all the members of the community. It is this feature of moral ascriptions that has encouraged many to remove them from that very reality with which scientific inquiry is concerned, the reality that addresses "how things are." Arthur Fine puts it succinctly:

> For realism, science is *about* something; something *out there,* "external" and (largely) independent of us. The traditional conjunction of externality and independence leads to the realist picture of an objective, external world; what I shall call the *World.* According to realism, science is about *that.* Being about the *World* is what gives significance to science.[5]

The methods and findings of the natural sciences are so considerable and broadly applicable as to raise serious questions about the reality of anything alleged to fall beyond their reach. Nonetheless, "natural sciences" is a term covering a remarkably wide range. Across this range the thick book of facts often conceals philosophically arguable assumptions. Moreover, not every fact as such finds a perfectly proportioned niche within the framework of scientific understandings. Not every fact bears directly or even by implication on the large and indubitable affairs of life. In yet another way, the very framing of the issue as one pitting facts against values—one pitting natural science against moral science—begs the central question. The central question, of course, is whether the last word on all matters of real, abiding significance is to be supplied by the natural sciences.

Reductionistic explanations so integral to the scientific program have strong and worthy support within philosophy of science, but also strong and worthy opposition within philosophy at large. What makes certain properties of reality interesting often includes elements

---

5. Arthur Fine, "The Natural Ontological Attitude," in *Scientific Realism,* ed. J. Leplin (Berkeley: University of California Press, 1984), p. 150.

which, if "reduced," are no longer explicable in terms that match up with reality itself. What makes the Battle of Waterloo a *battle* is not recoverable from even the most detailed account of the physiology and biochemistry of the participants. As William Dray made clear decades ago, significant historical events are *sui generis,* not suited to modes of explanation based on a repeated-measures paradigm, and utterly lost once reduced to a collection of corpuscular interactions. The Battle of Waterloo is no less "real" for being incompatible with reductionistic analyses or covering-law modes of explanation.

Nor is the incompatibility a sign of ambiguous ontological standing. It is instead a measure of the variegated nature of the reality with which the human understanding must contend. The tools forged by the human imagination include those of science itself. There is no user's manual able to declare in advance just which tool is not only the right but only one for the multitude of problems arising from the complexities of real life as really lived. Accordingly, it is less hubristic than absurd to dismiss as somehow *unreal* the entire class of facts, events, and phenomena transparently inaccessible to reductionistic forms of analysis and explanation.

The patent difference between physical and moral entities leaves little doubt but that the two cannot be expected to "fit into" the same ontological framework. This, however, cuts both ways, for no one seriously proposes eliminating the domain of physically real entities on the grounds that they fail to reflect moral properties. And if the incompatibility creates an unavoidable dualism, so be it. Simplicity, which is inevitably protean when invoked as a standard of explanation or, for that matter, taste, might usefully be contrasted with *complexity* as understood in systems theory. The complexity of a system is expressed by the number of sentences required to account fully for the operation of the system. On this understanding, any moral theory achieving simplicity would be suspect on its face. In all, then, it seems clear that the moral realist is able to defend the theory against criticisms based on positivistic assumptions expressly ruled out by the very nature of moral reality.

Turning now to the notorious FACT/VALUE rift, is it the case that moral statements or claims are not entailed by descriptive statements of fact? This is a question riddled with subtleties. It might be understood as arising from the stock assertion of the moral skeptic; viz., *there are no moral facts as such*. If, indeed, there simply are no moral facts, then clearly no descriptive statement of fact can include a moral fact among its entailments. The general argument might be understood in a more subtle way. Thus: *how could evidence at the level of direct perception entail what cannot be known at that level or even reached by inferences from one level to another?* In this form, however, the question would appear to ground a skepticism far too broad to be credible, and surely no more destructive of moral claims than of any number of non-moral but objective facts of daily life. To wit:

How could evidence, in the form of factual description, entail that the musculoskeletal events displayed by the nine bodies distributed on the grassy field constitute the game of baseball?

And, of course, the answer is not that the musculoskeletal events *entail* the game of baseball but just *constitute* it. The moral realist need not find an entailment rule by which to reach moral properties, given physical properties. The moral realist need only argue that, comprehended properly, some occurrences are by their nature *moral,* though in some other sense also embodied.

If the question actually is predicated on the assumption that there are no moral facts as such, one has good reason to ask whether that very assumption supports skeptical conclusions regarding architecture (there are no Gothic cathedrals *as such*), national borders (there is no France *as such*), etc. The point here is this: *arguments for moral realism are under no special burden in the matter of non-inferential truth claims.* In countless instances, an actuarial account of all that is directly perceived at the level of descriptive fact will fail to turn up what any competent observer comprehends immediately: games, battles, strategies, possessions, gifts.

Whether or not a complete description of the natural world can be rendered in exclusively physical terms is a metaphysical question of great subtlety. Common throughout the animal kingdom, at least as early in the phylogenetic series as the flatworm, is one or another sort of "dwelling." For some species the dwelling is within its own shell; others actually build such places. Although all such structures are physically describable, it is questionable whether even an exhaustive physical account conveys what it is that makes a physical entity a "dwelling." Even if such an account were produced, it is unquestionable but that it would fail to convey all that is readily conveyed by the notion of a "dwelling." Thus, although dwellings are utterly natural facts, they are not readily reducible to a congeries of fixed physical attributes. Presumably, such entities could be recognized as dwellings only by creatures who have—dwellings! Yet it would be odd to insist that, because of this, the concept of a dwelling is purely "subjective." It would be comparably odd to dismiss dwellings as objective facts on the grounds that they vary culturally, historically, and under different contextual pressures.

Finally, what has the moral realist to say to those who would locate moral values within the domain of purely cultural aims and habits? To begin, there are good reasons for doubting the adequacy of sociological and psychological conceptions of moral appraisals. These conceptions seem uniquely disabled before the task of explaining *moral progress.* The success of such movements as abolitionism and universal suffrage expresses something radically different from a mere tilting of majorities in one or another direction. In this same vein, the thesis that would have morality "socially constructed" whole cloth, with no more than local tools and resources, seems to be seriously flawed once its originating premises are considered, for these very premises leave little or no room for precisely that moral criticism *from within* that causes whole movements of thought and action. And, the connected thesis that would have "objectivity" somehow at variance with moral purposes is comparably defective, for objectivity itself is an essentially *moral* disposition. As for the phrase "how things are," it is by no means out of place when referring to moral precepts, and to lives in which actions and principles are coherently related. In a word, *the moral dimension of life is an integral feature of how things are.*

Note that it is not in virtue of a judgment being shared "conventionally" that it lapses into the "subjective" mode. The term "subjective" may be applied to opinions or perceptions that are merely *personal,* but not to those shared by nearly every member of the species. It is easy to be misunderstood on this point, for it is always tempting to beg this sort of question by assuming that the only "natural kinds" are unitary objects, inevitably and exhaustively defined in physical terms. It is, of course, unwarranted to conclude from the fact that something is the subject of experience that the "something" is subjective. Most of the facts, events, and measurements integral to the developed sciences are "subjects of experience" but no less real for that. And, as noted, a large number of facts in the natural world of living, breeding, competing, cohabiting species are not only subjects of experience but intelligible only to creatures possessing kindred inclinations and adaptations.

It may be asked of the moral realist whether moral properties are to be understood as "natural kinds," in the sense that animals, comets, and water are "natural kinds." The challenge implicit in the question arises from what seems to be wide cultural and historical variations in conceptions of good and evil. Whether moral entities ("good," "bad," etc.) are real in the sense of being instances of *natural kinds* depends on what one requires of natural kinds, and on this issue there is no settled position. Are species distinct and thus instances of a specific natural kind? What criteria are taken to be dispository in matters of this sort? Alexander Bird highlights the difficulty:

When one visits a greengrocer, in the section devoted to fruit one will find, among other things, apples, strawberries, blackcurrants, rhubarb, and plums, while the vegetable display will present one with potatoes, cabbages, carrots, tomatoes, peppers, and peas. If one were to ask a botanist to classify these items we will find rhubarb removed from the list of fruit and tomatoes and peppers added . . . Following this line . . . one might conclude that there really is no absolute sense in which there is a natural classification of things into kinds.[6]

What is indubitable is that there are apples, rhubarb, etc., which is to say that these names refer to entities that are reliable subjects of experience. They are no less reliable (and *real*) as subjects of experience for being difficult to classify in an undeviatingly consistent way. At a common sense level, one would say that the term "apple" ranges over a variety of items with a set of attributes understood to be required if the term is to be applied correctly. Apples have a *nominal essence* that includes their shape and color, their taste and size, etc. Actions and events routinely described as morally "good" or "bad" also have common properties and are classified, if not as consistently as apples are, with sufficient intersubjective reliability to qualify as having a *nominal essence.*

This is not to say that for anything to qualify as really existing it must have an abiding and universally recognized nominal essence. Consider only Saul Kripke's tiger critique: to say that the tiger has a nominal essence that includes "large, quadrupedal, carnivorous, black and yellow cat populous in India"—and that this qualifies tigers as a natural kind—is to fall prey to epistemic credulity. After all, those who were the first to see such creatures may have had defective vision, or may have seen only the few tigers who actually eat meat, or may even have failed to see a fifth leg on half the specimens. The point, of course, is that descriptions, no matter how consistent, are fallible accounts of *what is there* and cannot, therefore, be the last word on the nominal essence of a thing.[7] By the same token, the very complexity of moral events lends them to a wider range of descriptions, each perhaps focused more on one cluster of features than on another. As descriptive consistency does not guarantee a correct *essentialist* account,

---

6. Alexander Bird, *Philosophy of Science* (London: UCL Press, 1998), pp. 96–97.

7. Saul Kripke, *Naming and Necessity* (Cambridge, Mass.: Harvard University Press, 1980).

neither does descriptive inconsistency rule out the possibility that the described entities are natural and *real*.

All this will strike many here today as—shall I say it?—"merely philosophical." But it is not only philosophers who have wondered about the reference of evaluative descriptions. It was a matter of great interest to psychologists in the *Gestalt* tradition. If the core precept of *Gestalt* psychology is that *the whole is different from the sum of its parts,* then events perceived as having or embodying values offer suggestive examples. A passage from Wolfgang Köhler is instructive:

> Value may reside in the most varied classes of things. A dress may look elegant or sloppy, a face hard or weak, a street cheerful or dismal, and in a tune there may be morose unrest or quiet power. I admit, one's own self is among the entities in which values may reside. Such is the case when we feel fit or, at another time, moody. But the thesis that it is always valuation as an act which imbues its object with value as a pseudoattribute is perhaps nowhere more artificial than precisely in this instance. Here the self would have to equip itself with value attributes such as fitness or utter fatigue. The idea seems slightly fantastic. And if in this instance a thing per se manages to have value characteristics, why should we deny this possibility where other percepts are concerned?[8]

It is, indeed, fantastic to assume that a percipient possesses a set of attributes such as, say, "fatigue," then deploys these (even inaccurately) as a way of describing some otherwise incompletely comprehended event, such as one's fatigue. Rather, the ascriptions reach something resident in the "thing per se," as Köhler says, as that something is registered in the process of perception itself. The clam withdrawing into its shell in response to a threat in the external environment is using the shell as a protective dwelling, which it is, and this property, the property of *being-a-dwelling,* is as much in the shell as is calcium. The same is the case when, in our modes of most discerning compre-

8. Wolfgang Köhler, "Value and Fact," *Journal of Philosophy* 41 (1944): pp. 197–212.

hension, we examine the facts of the complex social world and reach judgments as to their moral features.

And, finally, the point of this disquisition? It is to encourage the thoughtful, the teaching and the reading classes, to re-examine the sense they confer on moral terms; to consider that, in the use of such terms, they may actually be reaching or attempting to reach really existing properties, the reality of which would obtain even if there were no one searching for them, let alone finding them. Here I offer encouragement to us all to approach the moral domain as we would other realms of reality, not sidetracked into thinking that our inquiries are the stuff of local tastes and village prejudice. We may well be wrong in classifying what we discover, but not because there are no real moral properties; only because, even in our most discerning modes of comprehension, we are seeking to uncover the most elusive of real properties which, for all we now know, may be as much a species of beauty as it is of truth.

three

Robert P. George

THE CONCEPT OF PUBLIC MORALITY

PUBLIC morals, like public health and safety, are a concern that goes beyond considerations of law and public policy. Public morality is affected, for good or ill, by the activities of private (in the sense of "non-governmental") parties, and such parties have obligations in respect to it. The acts of private parties—indeed, sometimes even the apparently private acts of private parties—can and do have public consequences. And choices to do things that one knows will bring about these consequences, whether directly or indirectly (in any of the relevant senses of "directly" and "indirectly"), are governed by moral norms, including, above all, norms of justice. Such norms will often constitute conclusive reasons for private parties not to bring about harmful public consequences.

Let us for just a moment lay aside the issue of public morality and focus instead on matters of public health and safety. Even apart from laws prohibiting the creation of fire hazards, for example, individuals have an obligation to avoid placing persons and property in jeopardy of fire. Similarly, even apart from legal liability in tort for unreasonably subjecting people to toxic pollutants, companies are under an obligation in justice to avoid freely spewing forth, say, carcinogenic smoke from their facilities. Concerns for public health and safety are, to be sure, justificatory grounds of criminal and civil laws; but they also ground moral obligations that obtain even apart from laws or in their absence.

What is true of public health and safety is equally true of public morals. Take, as an example, the problem of pornography. Material designed to appeal to the prurient interest in sex by arousing carnal desire unintegrated with the procreative and unitive goods of marriage, where such material flourishes, damages a community's moral ecology in ways analogous to those in which carcinogenic smoke spewing from a factory's stacks damages the community's physical ecology.

The central harm of pornography is not, as some people—especially some American judges—seem to suppose, that it shocks and offends people, any more than the central harm of carcinogenic smoke is that it smells bad. Rather, the central harm of pornography is moral harm—harm to character, and thus to the human goods and institutions, such as the good and institution of marriage, that are preserved and advanced by the disposition to act uprightly, and damaged and defiled by a contrary disposition, in respect to them. So the analogy is with the harmful impact of carcinogenic pollutants on the physical health of people subjected to them. And just as companies have an obligation in justice quite apart from considerations of legal liability to avoid damaging people's health by polluting the air, so too people have an obligation in justice even apart from legal prohibition to avoid harming people's character (and the goods and institutions that depend on widespread good character) by disseminating and making available to them pornographic materials.

Of course, an objection will immediately be raised. Pornography, it will be said, is quite unlike toxic environmental pollutants, even if it is true that pornography is morally bad in the way I have asserted. The difference is that members of a community *cannot* avoid breathing carcinogens that are spewed forth by a factory's smokestacks (except by leaving town); but they *can* avoid the morally harmful effects of pornography simply by declining to purchase and look at it. So, the argument goes, environmental polluters *really* do an injustice in spewing carcinogenic and other toxic pollutants into the air; pornographers, however, do no injustice to those who, after all, freely choose to subject themselves to their offerings. (This counterargument is ordinarily raised in connection with the question whether *laws* against pornography are justified, but I'm considering it here simply on its own merits and, for the moment, apart from questions of legal regulation.)

I don't think this counterargument works. First of all, it can be, and often is, unjust to subject people to powerful temptations to do things that are harmful to them, morally or otherwise, and whether or not they are cognizant of the harm. It seems to me mere (however widespread) liberal superstition to hold otherwise. Second, and even more importantly, the accumulation of private decisions to use pornography, as it impacts those who choose to use it, affects—sometimes profoundly—the community as a whole. For example, where pornography flourishes, as it does in our own culture, it erodes important shared public understandings of sexuality and sexual morality on which the health of the institutions of marriage and family life in any culture vitally depend. This is a classic case in which the accumulation of apparently private choices of private parties has big public consequences.

So, the pornographer, though a private party, fails in respect of his duties in justice to public morality, just as the environmental polluter—ordinarily motivated by the same consideration, that is, money—fails in respect of his duties to public health. And pornographers are not alone among the private parties whose unjust actions damage public morality: people who write and pose for pornographic publications and films, people who distribute pornography and make it available in newsstands, bookstores, theaters, and video shops, and, notably, people who purchase pornography (thus sustaining the industries that produce and disseminate it), and even those who in noncommercial contexts circulate it to friends, fellow workers, etc.

Well, there is much more to be said about pornography and public morality, and I will say a little more later in relation to a particular species of liberal argument against public morals legislation. I introduce the subject here only for purposes of illustrating the first point I wanted to make: namely, that public morality is not simply an issue about what laws we should have. Nor is it a concern that has no bearing on the moral deliberations and obligations of private parties, as opposed to public officials. The common good of public morality, that is, the good of a healthy moral ecology, generates obligations in justice for all of us, just as do the common goods of public health and safety.

Now let me make a second point, namely, that law and government play a secondary (or "subsidiary") role in upholding public morality. The primary role is played by families, churches, organizations such as the Boy Scouts, and other institutions that, by working closely with individuals, inculcate an understanding of morality and promote virtue. Despite the fact that public morality is a public good, its maintenance depends far more on contributions of private institutions than on those of law and government. Where families, churches, and other so-called institutions of "civil society" fail (or are unable) to play their parts, laws will hardly suffice to preserve public morals. Ordinarily, at least, law's role is to *support* families, churches, and the like. And, of course, law goes wrong when it displaces these institutions and usurps their authority. At the same time, the role of law in upholding public morality is undermined by families, churches, and other institutions who abdicate their responsibilities or, even worse, promote false and morally destructive practices.

Consider the current turmoil over marriage. If, as I believe, the good of marriage and its institutional integrity in our society depend on a firm understanding of, and public commitment to, marriage as a sexual union of one man and one woman, then a threat to marriage can come either from bad public policy or the misguided actions of key non-governmental associations (or both). On the one hand, law and public policy, in the name of a false neutrality, could undermine marriage by authorizing as marriages or their equivalent intrinsically non-marital (e.g., same-sex or polygamous) sexual relationships. In so doing, law and policy would make it immeasurably more difficult for families, churches, and other institutions of civil society to fulfill their primary role in upholding public morals in respect to marriage. On the other hand, even where the law maintains a sound doctrine of marriage, the institutional integrity of marriage could be gravely damaged by, for example, churches that, in the name of whatever moral or theological principle, bless same-sex or polygamous unions, or companies that treat employees' non-marital sexual partners as "spouses."

Of course, the validity of what I am saying about marriage *per se* entirely depends on whether I am right about its true nature. However, my point about public morality holds even if I'm wrong about marriage. Suppose I *am* wrong. Suppose that the true understanding of marriage extends to a range of possibilities including same-sex and polygamous relationships, and that it is mere bigotry that stands in the way of my perceiving this truth. In that case, public morals regarding marriage can be damaged either by laws unreasonably restricting marriage (as did anti-miscegenation laws that both reflected and reinforced racism in an earlier day) or by churches whose theologies and disciplines pertaining to marriage embody and promote bigotry.

Well, that is the sum and substance of what I have to say here about the obligations in justice of private parties to avoid damaging public morality and the primary role and responsibility of non-governmental institutions in inculcating virtue and, thus, upholding public morals. I hope that what I've said helps to elucidate the concept of public morality by detaching it from the question of law's part in protecting it. Now, however, I want to turn to that much debated question.[1]

As traditionally conceived, the "police powers" of governments of general jurisdiction extend to the protection and advancement of public health, safety, *and morals*. Particularly in the American setting, where, as a constitutional matter, power is shared between state governments of general jurisdiction and a national government of delegated and enumerated powers, it is important to bear in mind the distinction between the two. Governments of the former sort exercise police powers, including the police power to protect and promote public morals; governments of the latter sort do not, except to the extent that such governments are constitutionally empowered to act in a certain domain to combat particular threats to public health, safety, and morals.

What is meant by governments of "general jurisdiction"? Such governments are constitutionally empowered to act by way of legislation, regulation, etc. to preserve and advance the common good of the polities they serve, subject only to limitations constitutionally imposed on the scope of their power. (Of course, such empowerment and limitations are in some cases expressly set forth in written constitutions. In other cases, however, they are either implied by written constitutions or take the form of unwritten constitutional principles.)

In the United States, the governments of the states are, in form, at least, governments of general jurisdiction. They exercise police powers legally subject only to state or federal constitutional limitations on the scope of their authority. So, for example, in Massachusetts and other states whose constitutions include so-called "Blaine Amendments," state governments are disempowered from using public funds

---

1. I've written at length about this question in *Making Men Moral: Civil Liberties and Public Morality* (Oxford: Clarendon Press, 1993) and *In Defense of Natural Law* (Oxford: Oxford University Press, 2001), and will avoid repetition here to the extent possible.

to support religiously affiliated primary and secondary schools. In addition to such state constitutional limits on the powers of state governments, the Constitution of the United States imposes certain limits: for example, Article One, Section Ten forbids states from entering into treaties, granting letters of marque and reprisal, coining money, granting titles of nobility, passing bills of attainder, ex post facto laws, and laws impairing the obligation of contracts. In addition to these express limitations, the Supreme Court of the United States claims to have discovered in the federal constitution implied limitations of the police powers of states that forbid them from, for example, prohibiting or significantly restricting abortion, limiting what a candidate can spend from his own resources on a political campaign, and making it an offense to desecrate the American flag. Whatever one thinks of the validity of these rulings, it is plain that in the absence of express or implied constitutional limitations, the State of Indiana, for example, as a government of general jurisdiction, would be legally empowered to support religious schools, release people from contractual obligations, grant titles of nobility, limit campaign spending, restrict abortion, prohibit flag desecration, etc.

In this respect, the governments of the states differ markedly—again, in form, at least—from the government of the United States. The latter government is not a government of general jurisdiction; it is not constitutionally authorized to exercise police powers. On the contrary, it is a government of delegated and enumerated powers. Where the states are *generally* authorized to act for the sake of the common good, enjoying the authority to act *except* to the extent that their jurisdiction is constitutionally limited, the federal government may, as a constitutional matter, act *only where it has been constitutionally delegated the power to act*. Again, this delegation can be express or implied. Article One, Section Eight of the Constitution of the United States expressly delegates to the Congress power to coin money, for example, to establish a Post Office, to declare war, to create armies and a navy, and do various other things. The same section authorizes Congress to "make all Laws necessary and proper for carrying into Execution the foregoing Powers . . . ." So, the Supreme Court long ago held that the chartering by Congress of a national bank, though nowhere mentioned among the enumerated powers of the national government, was "necessary and proper" to the execution of certain powers expressly delegated to that government by the Constitution. So, too, we must suppose, the power to create and maintain a welfare system and a system of social security. Again, for our purposes it doesn't matter whether one agrees with the Court's rather expansive interpretation of the implied powers of the government of the United States. The point is that, as a government of delegated powers, the United States may lawfully do *only* those things that it is—expressly or impliedly—constitutionally empowered to do.

Since the Constitution originally contained no authorization of federal income taxation without apportionment among the several states, proponents of the income tax found it necessary to amend the Constitution, as they succeeded in doing in 1913, to confer this power on the national government. However desirable its proponents judged the income tax to be as a means of preserving or enhancing the welfare of the nation, they could not simply put an income tax bill through Congress. It was necessary for them first to bring into being by amendment a constitutional delegation of the power to impose the tax. Likewise the prohibition of intoxicating liquors. Prior to the ratification of the Eighteenth Amendment to the Constitution in 1919, the federal government, lacking police powers, had no authority to regulate or prohibit the sale of alcoholic beverages. One year after ratification, according to the terms of the amendment, "the manufacture, sale, or transportation of intoxicating liquors within, the importation thereof into, or the exportation thereof from the United States" was constitutionally prohibited, and Congress was empowered to legislate concurrently with the states to enforce this constitutional prohibition. There the matter rested until a thirsty America effected repeal of the Eighteenth Amendment by the Twenty-First in 1933. Repeal,

in turn, restored public policy decisions regarding regulation of alcoholic beverages to the states, which, as governments of general jurisdiction, were free to exercise their police powers as they saw fit to
regulate (and even prohibit) alcohol in the interests of public health,
safety, and morals.

Of course, the century just concluded witnessed a massive expansion of the power of the national government, largely at the expense
of the states. Formal constitutional amendment, as with the income
tax, is one way this happened. More often, however, the courts (after
some initial resistance in the New Deal era) and the American people as a whole simply acquiesced in the federal government's claims
to be exercising implied delegated powers (as, for example, with the
federal welfare and social security systems). As we enter the new century, the delegated powers doctrine, as a limitation on the jurisdiction of the national government, seems as false in practice as it is true
in theory. For all *practical* purposes, the government of the United
States functions as a government of general jurisdiction, more or less
freely exercising what can only be termed police powers. Of course,
the formalities associated with the delegated powers doctrine continue to be observed: whenever, and for whatever reason, Congress acts,
it purports to do so under some power granted to it by the Constitution—ordinarily the power to regulate commerce among the several
states. True, the Supreme Court has found an occasion or two in the
last decade to invalidate acts of Congress as overstepping the delegated powers of the national government; by and large, however, the
federal government acts as a government of general jurisdiction constrained only by those limitations expressly or impliedly set forth in
the Constitution of the United States, such as provisions forbidding
the government from establishing religious tests for public office, prohibiting the free exercise of religion, abridging the freedom of speech,
conducting unreasonable searches and seizures, and imposing excessive fines.

The federal government's effective exercise of police powers is evident in a variety of areas of public health and safety. Federal environmental laws, occupational safety and health regulations, and so forth preempt state legislation across a vast swath of terrain and, for better or worse, affect all of us every day. Even in areas of public morality the federal government has taken on a role. The classic instance was the Mann Act, prohibiting the transportation of women across state lines for immoral purposes (that is, prostitution). Similarly, Congress has prohibited the use of the mails for the distribution of obscene materials, including child pornography, and is attempting, albeit so far unsuccessfully in the face of judicial resistance, to restrict children's access to indecent material on the Internet. And there are other examples.

Whether it is the federal or state governments exercising the police power to protect public morality, what is the nature of the power? As an abstract matter of political morality, what is its justification? Consideration of the specifics of contemporary American constitutional interpretation aside, what is its scope and what are its limits?

Let's return to the question I began to explore earlier: what is public morality? One way of understanding it is simply as morality—the moral uprightness of individual people and the associations they form—considered insofar as it is a public good. But morality of what sort? Political morality, that is, the principles and norms of right and wrong as they pertain to the establishment of a system of government and to the government's actions, is, in a rather obvious sense, a public good. It is certainly for the common good—indeed, it is a strict requirement of the common good of political society—that a just system of government be established and maintained and that the government act justly. But political morality is not what the government upholds—it is not the public good for whose sake a government of general jurisdiction acts—when it successfully exercises its police power to protect public morality. Public morals legislation does not regulate the government or governmental actors, as such. Rather, it regulates the behavior of individuals—citizens and those residing permanently or temporarily within the government's jurisdiction. It limits *their* choices and behaviors. But, insofar as these are private (that is to say, non-governmental) actors, in what sense do these regulations protect a public good?

As we have seen, public morals laws, like health and safety regulations, regulate private conduct insofar as it harms, or threatens to harm, the public interest. Now, here it is important to avoid confusion. Sometimes, the term "private," when used to describe or classify conduct, is meant to indicate conduct that does not bear on the public interest, or which is not legitimately subject to government prohibition or restriction even if it does affect the public interest. The term thus figures in accounts of, or arguments about, political morality. Typically, it is invoked as part of a claim about the alleged injustice of certain acts of government that, say, violate the right of the individual against certain forms of regulation—including morals laws. Such laws, it is commonly asserted, violate citizens' "constitutional liberty," or "right to privacy," or "right to moral independence," or what have you. Obviously, this is not how I am here using the term. Rather, I use it to refer to conduct by individuals or groups acting as private parties, as opposed to those exercising the power of the state.

Now this is not to suggest that the actions of governments cannot harm public morality. Nothing could be further from the truth. And I have in mind here not merely the failure of government prudently to act where it can to protect public morality against the damaging acts of private parties.

That is certainly one thing. Another thing, however, is government action that itself positively undermines public morals by, for example, encouraging and facilitating immoral acts by private citizens. If prostitution, for example, is, as I believe it to be, a wicked practice, then local governments in the Netherlands undermine public morality by (assuming, as I do with the greatest caution, that the *New York Times* is to be believed) providing free prostitutes to physically disabled (though evidently not too physically disabled) men (and, I have no doubt, women) who request them. But, of course, no government is going to legislate against its own bad moral judgments. However bizarre the Dutch policy, it would be even more peculiar to find the Dutch government enacting morals legislation to prohibit the Dutch government from providing prostitutes (though there wouldn't be anything odd about the people of the Netherlands, were they so inclined, constitutionally prohibiting their government from getting up to such shenanigans). If the Dutch government saw the thing rightly from the moral point of view, there would be no need for legislation; it would simply discontinue the policy of providing prostitutes.

Staying with the example of prostitution—a classic subject of morals laws—let us think further about what public good is damaged, what public harm is done, by the provision of prostitutes, whether by governments in the grip of sexual liberationist ideology or private businessmen motivated by greed.

Assuming, again, that prostitution is indeed immoral, then the availability of prostitutes is going to facilitate immoral acts by individuals—prostitutes and their customers. Of course, the commercial sex acts will likely take place in "private," that is, behind closed doors, and it could be the case that there is no highly visible publicizing of the prostitutes' availability (though unless there is some way of getting the word out publicly, there won't be much work for the prostitutes). Still, *public* interests are damaged. The public has an interest in men not engaging prostitutes: for when they do, they damage their own characters; they render themselves less solid and reliable as husbands and fathers; they weaken their marriages and their ability to enter into good marriages and authentically model for others (including their children) the virtue of chastity on which the integrity of marriages and of marriage as an institution in any given society depends; they set bad examples for others. In short, they damage what I have referred to as the community's "moral ecology"—an ecology as vital to the community's well-being, and, as such, as integral to the public interest, as the physical ecology which is protected by, for example, environmental laws enacted pursuant to the police powers to protect public health.

Now, the question arises as to the scope of the police power to protect public morality. Much of what I've said about the harm of prostitution applies equally to fornication and adultery. And, to be sure, public morals legislation has traditionally forbidden these vices, just as it has forbidden prostitution. However, some people argue that while the legal prohibition of prostitution is legitimately within the scope of the police powers, the prohibition of fornication and adultery are not. The latter vices, however wicked and destructive of important public interests, are truly private, at least insofar as they are engaged in by consenting adults. Apparently, the view is that it is the commercial aspect of prostitution that makes the immoral acts of consenting adults in this case an issue of *public,* as opposed to purely *private,* morality.

It is, of course, true that prostitutes and their pimps are inviting and doing business with "the public" in a way that ordinary fornicators and adulterers are not. And I can certainly see how this distinction could be relevant to the prudential reasoning of legislators considering enactment or repeal of legal prohibitions of non-commercial sexual vice. What I cannot see, however, is the ground for claiming *that a strict principle of justice* excludes the criminal prohibition of non-commercial sexual vice. The reasons for prohibition—namely the protection of a community's moral ecology against the corrosive effects on marriage and family life of vices such as fornication and adultery—may be defeated by competing prudential considerations; but where they are not defeated by such considerations, no principle of justice of which I am aware provides a trumping reason.

Needless to say, a great many people believe the contrary. Some doubt that there is anything morally wrong with any form of sex act between consenting adults. Where there is no coercion or, perhaps, dishonesty involved, they find nothing morally objectionable against prostitution, much less adultery and fornication. If such acts tend to undermine the institutions of marriage and the family, as these institutions are traditionally understood, then so much the worse for these institutions. These institutions are, in any event, in need of transformation, partisans of sexual liberation insist, in light of a new, "uninhibited," more "enlightened" and "inclusive" morality. Well, perhaps you will excuse my ignoring people who see things this way for present purposes. If they are correct, then traditional public morals legislation, at least insofar as it pertains to what has been considered sexual vice, is misguided at its root. And the reason for not enforcing by law traditional concepts of sexual morality is that these concepts are themselves unsound. Of course, I think people who suppose that prostitution, adultery, fornication, and the like are morally innocent are profoundly mistaken, and I have set forth my reasons for so thinking at great length in various publications.[2] I won't repeat my arguments here.

The more interesting moral criticisms of the criminal prohibition of vices like adultery and fornication come from people who agree, or are, at least, willing to grant for the sake of argument, that these are in fact vices. The most familiar form of argument along these lines appeals to the idea of a basic individual moral right to "autonomy," "privacy," "moral independence," or what have you. Why is it allegedly wrong to criminalize fornication? Because, it is asserted, people have a right to fornicate—a "moral right to do wrong." Perhaps this is because fornication is a "private" matter. The trouble here, though, is that fornication is one of those vices that, when widely practiced, tolerated, and, inevitably, accepted, has very big and very public consequences—consequences that provide a perfectly intelligible reason for legal proscription, or, short of that, non-coercive public efforts to discourage it.

2. See *In Defense of Natural Law,* chs. 8, 9, 15, and 16. See also John Finnis, "Law, Morality, and 'Sexual Orientation,'" *Notre Dame Law Review* 69 (1994) and "The Good of Marriage and the Morality of Sexual Relations," *American Journal of Jurisprudence* 42 (1997).

To his credit, Ronald Dworkin candidly acknowledges that apparently private vices—including vices, such as pornography, to which he believes people have a moral right—can and do damage the public interest. And Dworkin does not propose to derive rights to such vices from a general right to liberty or autonomy. He doesn't believe in any such general right. Government restricts liberty and autonomy all the time without touching upon, much less violating, anybody's rights. For Dworkin, it is a basic right to equality—a right of individuals to be treated by government with equal concern and respect—that grounds a right of moral independence that provides the principled, moral reason for government to refrain from criminalizing pornography (or, a Dworkinian might easily argue, adultery, fornication, even prostitution) despite its harm to the public interest.[3]

Dworkin maintains that government violates the basic right to equal concern and respect when it restricts liberty, on the ground that one citizen's conception of what makes for or detracts from a valuable and morally worthy way of life is superior to another citizen's conception. For example, in forbidding pornography, the government limits Larry Flynt's liberty—unjustly, by hypothesis—on the ground that Billy Graham's view of whether pornography is wicked or harmless is the correct one. Of course, Dworkin does not claim that the government's error is in supposing that there *is* a right answer to the moral question of pornography, or even that it is Graham, rather than Flynt, who has the right answer. Indeed, he candidly—and rightly—concedes that pornography, where it is permitted to flourish, makes the community worse off in very concrete moral respects, namely, it

> sharply limit[s] the ability of individuals consciously and reflectively to influence the conditions of their own and their children's development. It . . . limit[s] their ability to bring about the cultural structure that they think best, a structure in which sexual experience in general

3. Dworkin sets forth his view most fully in "Do We Have a Right to Pornography?" in *A Matter of Principle* (Cambridge, Mass.: Harvard University Press, 1985).

has dignity and beauty, without which their own and their families' experience are likely to have these qualities in less degree.[4]

As I say, Dworkin is right to concede what he concedes about the way in which pornography (and we might add other forms of sexual vice) damages the community's moral ecology—and thus the public interest. The trouble is that, having made these concessions, his argument from the principle of equality falls apart. The basic problem is that legislators and other officials who act on the proposition that pornography, for example, is damaging to the community in the way Dworkin concedes it is, are not judging between Larry Flynt and Billy Graham, or even the moral convictions of Larry Flynt and Billy Graham *inasmuch as they are Flynt's and Graham's*. They are acting, assuming (as Dworkin does) that they are responsible, conscientious officials, on *their* best judgment as to whether and how pornography is bad. They are not banning pornography because *Flynt is for it and/ or Graham is against it.* Nor does Dworkin imagine that that is *why* they are banning it. As he is perfectly aware, the fact that the judgment that pornography is morally bad and destructive of the common good is Graham's (or Dworkin's or mine) is *of no particular relevance* to the officials' deliberations. They are interested in reasons and arguments—not individuals. In judging the anti-pornography view to be sound and the pro-pornography view to be unsound, they are, to be sure, treating *positions* as other than equal (and inasmuch as these positions are held by people, one might say, at some small risk of misleading, that they are treating *different people's positions unequally*). But insofar as it is the *positions* as such being judged, they are in no way treating *people—including the people holding the positions— unequally.* So, although I agree with Dworkin that government has an obligation in justice to treat those under its authority with equal concern and respect, I find no violation of this principle in laws against pornography, prostitution, adultery, fornication, and the like.

4. Dworkin, *A Matter of Principle,* p. 349.

In his recent work, John Finnis has proposed a principled moral limit to the authority of the state to enforce morality.[5] Finnis's argument is far less sweeping in its scope than Dworkin's, and he entirely eschews the anti-perfectionism that Dworkin's thought shares with other orthodox liberal approaches to the question. It does not appeal to alleged rights to privacy, autonomy, liberty, or moral independence as grounds for limitation on governmental authority to criminalize immoral behavior; and only in the most highly attenuated and strictly limited sense can it be said to license a moral right to do moral wrong, that is, a right to be free of governmental interference with the strictly private immoral acts of consenting adults. Nothing in Finnis's argument implies or entails the "expressive individualism," and accompanying elements of relativism, characteristic of liberal political theories.

The premise of Finnis's argument is that the common good of the political community is, fundamentally, an instrumental, rather than an intrinsic, constitutive, and, as such, basic, human good. This is not to suggest that the political common good is unimportant or dispensable. On the contrary, Finnis recognizes that care of the political common good is profoundly important to the well-being of human persons and the associations they form —including associations, such as the family and church, whose common good is itself intrinsic and *not* merely instrumental. Moreover, the political common good is "great and godlike," to quote Aristotle, in its profoundly ambitious range, which is, Finnis says, "to secure the whole ensemble of . . . conditions to favour, facilitate, and foster the realization by each individual of his or her personal development."[6] Thus, political authority legitimately extends even to the regulation, within limits, "of friendships, marriage, families, and religious associations, as well as all the many or-

5. See, for example, John Finnis, "Is Natural Law Theory Compatible with Limited Government?" in *Natural Law, Liberalism, and Morality,* ed. Robert P. George (Oxford: Clarendon Press, 1996).

6. Finnis, "Is Natural Law Theory," p. 5.

ganizations and associations which, like the state itself, have only an instrumental common good."[7]

Still, inasmuch as the political common good *is* an instrumental good, Finnis argues, political authority is limited by the inherent limits of its general justifying aim: viz., to secure the social conditions of the well-being of individuals and their communities. So, he quotes from the teaching of the Second Vatican Council which, in its Declaration on Religious Freedom *(Dignitatis Humanae),* clearly affirms the instrumental quality of the political common good. Speaking of restrictions on religious liberty, the Declaration proposes that such restrictions are justified where required "for [1] the effective protection of the rights of all citizens and of their peaceful coexistence, [2] a sufficient care for the authentic public peace of an ordered common life in true justice, and [3] a proper upholding of public morality."

Now, as Finnis says, the Council's idea of public morality is precisely the preservation of a social environment conducive to virtue and inhospitable to at least the grosser forms of vice. This is not to say, however, that government may legitimately promote virtue and repress vice, *as such,* that is, *just for their own sakes,* at least via coercive means. Finnis does not claim that the Council expressly rules this sort of legal moralism and paternalism out of bounds; his claim is merely that "government is precisely not presented here as dedicated to the coercive promotion of virtue and the repression of vice, as such" (ibid., p. 6). I'm not sure whether the term "precisely" in Finnis's remark is doing any real work. Perhaps it is meant to suggest that the Council really did face the issue more or less squarely and did come down the way Finnis thinks we should come down once we've taken on board the implications for the scope of political authority of the fact that the common good of political society is an instrumental, rather than intrinsic, good. In any event, the key thing is that Finnis thinks that, having taken on board this fact, we should see that law and the state exceed their just authority—thus violating a principle

7. Ibid.

of justice—when they go beyond the protection of the public moral environment and criminalize "even secret and truly consensual adult acts of vice" (ibid., p. 8).

I disagree. Perhaps I'm blinded by what Joseph Boyle once described—in jest, I hope—as my "incorrigibly authoritarian impulses." Or perhaps I've caught John Finnis, in his great generosity of spirit, straining to find a kernel of wisdom in the liberal account of freedom and public morality. However it may be, let me note that the difference between Finnis and me, as a practical matter, is quite small. First of all, even in the absence of a principled limit to the authority of the state to enforce true moral obligations along the lines of the one Finnis proposes, it seems to me that there are often compelling prudential reasons for law to tolerate vices, lest efforts to eradicate them produce worse evils still.[8] Second, Finnis's position is hardly a liberal, much less a strictly libertarian, one. Unlike, say, Dworkin and other mainstream liberal political theorists, Finnis goes so far as to say that "the political community's rationale requires that its public managing structure, the state, should deliberately and publicly identify, encourage, facilitate, and support the truly worthwhile (including moral virtue), should deliberately and publicly identify, discourage and hinder the harmful and evil, and should by its criminal prohibitions and sanctions (as well as its other laws and policies) assist people with parental responsibilities to educate children and young people in virtue and to discourage their vices" (ibid.). Moreover, virtually the entire range of traditional morals legislation can and would be justified on grounds that fit well within Finnis's conception of the scope of the police power to uphold public morals. Laws against intrinsic evils such as prostitution, pornography, drug abuse, and the like, as well as those regulating gambling, alcohol, etc., are justified, in part, by a concern to protect the public environment in ways that Finnis's approach to the question does not exclude in principle.

8. This is Aquinas's position in *Summa theologiae* Ia-IIae q. 96, a. 1, and one that I have endorsed in all of my writings on the subject.

On the subject of moral paternalism, on which we disagree, I suspect that the difference between Finnis's position and mine is narrow. He would exclude *in principle*, and I would not, laws against "private" (e.g., non-commercial) fornication, adultery, and sodomy. But where he would permit regulation, as in prohibiting prostitution, shutting down bathhouses, criminalizing the sale of illicit drugs, etc., I suspect he would see any good paternalistic side effects of such state action as welcome. In other words, if I'm right, Finnis would not see paternalism as a valid justification for criminalization of a vice; but where criminalization is justified for other reasons, he would welcome good paternalistic consequences and would believe the state to be acting within its rightful authority in structuring its laws and activities to produce such consequences where possible. (What I have in mind here is analogous to the way in which some non-retributive goals of punishment systems—such as deterrence and rehabilitation—are welcome, and may rightly be sought, though, by themselves, they do not justify punishment, nor are they its central purpose.)

Why, then, do I resist Finnis's argument on the basic point? Two reasons: First, it doesn't follow, or so it seems to me, from the instrumental nature of the political common good that moral paternalism, where it can be effective, is beyond the scope of that good. Second, I think that the concept of truly secret vices is, when it comes to laws such as those pertaining to fornication, adultery, and sodomy, a very slippery and unsatisfactory one. "Secret" vices have a way of not staying secret. There may be good prudential reasons not to attack them with the full force of the law—and even where the law is employed, authorities should be careful not to employ excessive zeal in enforcing it—but that is not to say that, *as a matter of principle,* the law may not forbid them.

four

～

Hadley Arkes

THE MALADIES OF THE POLITICAL

CLASS *When Reasons Cease to Matter*

I HAVE argued for a long time that the comedians are really in the same business as the philosophers, for they both may make their livings by playing off the shades of meaning and logic built into the language. I used to say, in this vein, that my favorite epistemologist was Lou Costello, for there was the occasion when his partner, Bud Abbott, came up with a fine idea, and Costello said, "That's an excellent thought—I was just going to think of it myself." With that sense of the connection, I'd like to open into my problem by using my favorite show, *Guys and Dolls,* as the bridge to James Wilson, of Pennsylvania, who would rank among the preeminent minds of the American Founders.[1]

---

1. Wilson took a leading role in framing the Constitution; he became a member of the first Supreme Court, appointed by George Washington, and with Washington in at-

My bridge, as I say, is through *Guys and Dolls,* and that moment of acute embarrassment when Sky Masterson offers a wager to the gamblers joined in a crap game: he bets them each $1,000 against their souls. They will get $1,000 if he doesn't make his point, but if he wins they will have to attend a prayer meeting. Of course he wins, which produces much grumbling. On the way to the prayer meeting there is a vain protest made by Big Jule from Chicago, who had come packing heat, but who would later affirm that, while he had been bad as a youngster, he had now gone straight, as shown by his record: thirty-two arrests and no convictions. But Big Jule protests to Harry the Horse: if it ever gets back to Cicero, Illinois, his home base in Chicago—if the news ever gets out that he had attended a prayer meeting—then, as he says, "no decent person will speak to me."

The writers could count on the laughs, because they could count on the public understanding at once the inversion: only in the circles inhabited by Big Jule, with the code that prevails among his friends, could it be taken as the mark of suspicion—of possible defection, a falling away from rectitude—that a person would go to a prayer meeting. Now that is what the writers of *Guys and Dolls* treated as a joke— and counted on the fact that an audience, or a public, would regard as a joke. They assumed, that is, that no one could plausibly be "defamed," that no one's reputation could rightly be impaired, by the report that he respected a law outside himself. And that seemed especially apparent with that law proclaimed by the God who enjoined us not to murder (not to kill without justification); not to steal (not to appropriate, as our own, what belonged to others); or not to bear false witness (not to give a false account that wrongly injured the innocent). In other words, it was not conceivable that any law of defamation could coherently regard as a bad man—a man undeserving of the company of decent people—a man who lived under the restraint of respecting a law beyond his own appetite, respecting the per-

---

tendance he began his remarkable lectures on jurisprudence at the University of Pennsylvania in 1790.

son and property of others, and visiting no harm upon the innocent.

But to say these things is to make the point that James Wilson made in the course of his lectures on jurisprudence. When we face the question of defamation, we face the serious fact that people can genuinely be injured in their reputation—they can suffer the effects of decent people's shunning any commerce with them—if their character is impugned. But all of that presupposes, says Wilson, that we begin with an understanding of what constitutes impugning. As Wilson argued, any law of defamation would have to presuppose a rather fixed system of moral principles, describing the way of life that is in fact more rightful for human beings. To put it another way, "law" as "law" could not detach itself, in a posture of neutrality, and serve up a system of rules—say, a law of defamation, attached to just any moral code, such as the code that governed Big Jule from Chicago. Wilson recalled Montesquieu's contention that "honor" was the leading virtue or principle in monarchies, and that republics, with their leveling tendencies, rather disparaged the aristocratic pride and sense of honor. But Montesquieu also thought, as Wilson said, that honor can "subsist without honesty," for he had written that, in well-policed monarchies, there are very few honest men. Montesquieu's sense of the matter seemed closer to that of Joseph Addison when he wrote

> Honour's a sacred tie—
> The noble mind's distinguishing perfection,
> That aids and strengthens virtue, where it meets her . . .
> And imitates her actions, where she is not.[2]

But on that subtle and decisive point, Wilson thought Addison had it wrong: "The counterfeit of virtue," he said, "should not be dignified with the appellation of honour." Montesquieu readily understood that the honor flourished in monarchies could be displays without substance. As Wilson put it, "It is that honour which judges of actions not as they are good, but as they are showy; not as they are

2. Joseph Addison, *Cato: A Tragedy* (London: Longman, 1808).

just, but as they are grand; not as they are reasonable, but as they are extraordinary. It is, in one word, that honour, which fashions the virtues just as it pleases, and extends or limits our duties by its own whimsical taste."[3]

Honor, in the strictest sense, could not be reserved to monarchies. Every citizen in a republic, who could claim the protection of the law, had a stake in his honor and reputation, and no law of defamation could be built, as a whimsy, on just any moral code, or just any sense of honor. We may josh about the way in which Big Jule might have his reputation damaged in Chicago, but no law of defamation could coherently be built on the premises of relativism. Any law of defamation would have to take its bearings, or its standards of judgment, from that ancient understanding of the things that are higher and lower—the rather emphatic structure of moral judgment that arises from the logic of morals itself, or which flows, as Kant suggested, from the very idea of a "rational creature as such." To be sure, any law of defamation will have to be sensitive to local usage in the meaning of language. In some places, it may indeed be odious to be called a "snark" or a "boojum" or a Cubs fan—and in Germany, in the 20s and 30s, it was libelous to be known, wrongly, as a Jew. But the critical point, in the first place—which should not be missed—is that the logic of morals kicks in: if people are labeled as odious or blameworthy, the label is not usually followed by applause and by a showering of benefits. What is odious is shunned, reprobated, punished. Consistent with that logic, it could have been true for Big Jule that, if he had acquired a reputation as a churchgoer, he would have suffered ostracism and humiliation.

And yet, as Wilson argued, the law could never entirely accommodate that kind of local ethic. No law that deals with a reputation for goodness or badness could regard, as an actionable accusation,

3. James Wilson, "Of the Natural Rights of Individuals," in *The Works of James Wilson*, ed. Robert Green McCloskey (Cambridge, Mass.: Harvard University Press, 1967; originally published in 1804), vol. 2, pp. 585–610, at 594–95.

the complaint that "knowingly, deliberately, I was painted by my ad-
versary as a man of self-restraint, who always preferred some other
interest to his own." Or: "My reputation was blackened as the word
got about that I was one who persistently, incorrigibly, fulfilled his
promises and contracts." Or: "People shunned my company because I
was accused falsely of never shading the truth for the sake of my own
advantage, and because I was known to be insufferable in constantly
respecting a law beyond my own appetites."

The laws on defamation could not be entirely neutral on the kind
of character that was considered odious or blameworthy—unless the
laws were deeply corrupted, perhaps because they were outgrowths of
a regime that was corrupt in principle. In the Third Reich, it could indeed be actionable for libel to be identified, wrongly, as a Jew, much
as it was actionable under the laws in the American South to be identified, wrongly, as a Negro or black. But the laws on defamation in
these cases were reflections of corruptions in the laws themselves, and
the corruption of the laws was a possibility immanent in the notion
of polity itself. The polis began with an understanding of the rightful and wrongful ends of political life. The very notion of the polis
and law sprung from the nature of a certain kind of creature—that
creature who could not only conjugate verbs but give reasons over the
things that were right or wrong. As Aristotle said, in that critical passage, animals could emit sounds to indicate pleasure or pain, but humans could declare what was just and unjust.[4] Of course, that difference dissolved entirely if we translated the problem in the terms of
David Hume and understood the difference between the just and the
unjust as the difference between the things that gave us pleasure or
pain. In that event, to declare something unjust was hardly different
from emitting sounds to indicate that one found the event unpleasant
or displeasing.

The polis began then with an understanding of what was dis-

4. Aristotle, *Politics,* 1252a, in *The Complete Works of Aristotle,* ed. Jonathan Barnes
(Princeton, N.J.: Princeton University Press, 1984), p. 1986.

tinct to human nature, but in the same way, it began with a recognition of what was higher and lower in human beings. Higher than the knowledge, say, of how to be skillful with a knife was the knowledge of whether one was using that knife for ends that were justified or unjustified. The man who could respect, as I say, a law or a principle of rightness outside himself was higher, better, than a person who knew no law beyond his own wants. We meet at a time in which the academy has been pervaded by the premises of moral relativism, and yet, as Wilson and the Founders understood, our laws are permeated by the most emphatic understanding of the ways of life that are rightful or wrongful for human beings. And without that sense of things, the law becomes incoherent even for the votaries of the most precious theories of relativism.

Wilson sought to demonstrate that point at every turn, with virtually all dimensions of the law. To speak of the law is to speak at some point of trials, in assessing fault and blame and judging the aptness of punishment. But to respect the difference between the guilty and the innocent is to insist that we make those discriminations only in the most demanding way, with evidence and reasoning. As Lincoln pointed out, the crowd that chased a man down the street, caught him, and hanged him might well have punished the right man, but the way in which the thing was done was quite fearful. The rational weighing of evidence, the reasoned judgment on the truth or falsity of propositions, is in point of principle preferable to arbitrary modes of judgment—if we are indeed making judgments of innocence and guilt, with the consequence of inflicting punishments.

But Wilson raised the question, what constitutes "evidence"? And there he recognized that the question at the root was a question of epistemology. It was a question of how we can know anything reliably—and it was a question, once again, that presupposed a certain kind of creature, a creature with the faculty of *epistemonikon*, as Daniel Robinson would instruct us, the capacity to know universals. If we encountered that familiar biped, the man on the street, say in Brooklyn or Arlington, and he professed not to know that the statutes on theft encompassed bicycles and computers, it is a measure of the respect we tender that biped that we refuse to credit that complaint. Even if the laws on theft mention nothing of bicycles and computers, we evidently expect him to understand that if he takes what is not his own, without permission or justification, the theft is virtually indifferent to the thing that is stolen. We expect him, curiously, to understand that the principle covers virtually all the instances that may fit under the principle; and there is no need for law to spell out all of the instances.

That was a mark of what was strikingly curious, years ago, when the Supreme Court confronted a law in Virginia that barred marriage across racial lines, and Chief Justice Warren opened his opinion by saying that the Court had never encountered a case of this kind before.[5] Never before? The Court had never dealt with a case of racial discrimination, or had never dealt with regulations of marriage? The Court had not dealt with racial discrimination in marriage in the way it would now, but that was simply to say that, even in *Brown v. Board of Education,* the Court had never gotten clear on the principle that defines the wrong of racial discrimination. The "wrong" of Brown was cast in terms of an injury done to black children in schools; but then the Court would have a bit of trouble in explaining the wrong of racial discrimination in swimming pools, since discrimination there might not affect the performance of black children in school. If the Court had come to a recognition that racial discrimination was in principle wrong, then it might have recognized that the wrong in principle was quite indifferent to all of those instances in which the wrong could be manifested—whether in schools, swimming pools, tennis courts, or in the use of a public Xerox machine. I once mused over what the Court would have done if the law in Virginia had barred partnerships in business across racial lines, and a case had come up of two friends,

5. See *Loving v. Virginia,* 388 U.S. 1 (1967).

black and white, who bought a delicatessen (with the case called *Za-bar's v. Virginia*). When the Court struck down the law, would commentators on the law, looking back on the case, have said that the case established the right to own a delicatessen?[6] It made no more sense to describe *Loving v. Virginia* as establishing a "right to marry."

The curious thing is that the judges did not seem to grasp what we expect ordinary folks to know about the laws, in grasping the notion of a principle. Yet, when we expect ordinary people to grasp the sense of a principle—to recognize that the principle on theft would cover squash racquets and computers, even if these things are unmentioned in the statutes—we hold people responsible for things they cannot know simply through their senses. Wilson evidently had absorbed deeply the writings of Thomas Reid, and he shared Reid's dubiety about the empiricists of his age, the writers, notably Locke and Hume, who held that we drew our knowledge mainly through the senses, through the impressions that they made, say, on our hearing or touch. And so, by this construction, said Wilson, instead of knowing a person, we would have an impression or idea of a person.

> We have hitherto been apt, perhaps, with unphilosophic credulity, to imagine, that thought supposed a thinker; and that treason implied a traitor. But correct philosophy, it seems, discovers, that all this is a mistake; for that there may be treason without a traitor, laws without a legislator, punishment without a sufferer. If in these cases, the *ideas* are the traitor, the legislator, the sufferer; the author of this discovery ought to inform us, whether ideas can converse together; whether they can possess rights, or be under obligations; whether they can make promises, enter into covenants, fulfil or break them.[7]

In the first case that elicited a set of opinions from the Supreme Court, *Chisholm v. Georgia,* in 1793, Wilson acknowledged that we

6. For that discussion, see my book *First Things* (Princeton, N.J.: Princeton University Press, 1986), pp. 343–45.

7. Wilson, "Of Man as an Individual," in *The Works of James Wilson,* vol. 1, pp. 197–226, at 215; italics in the original.

were at the beginning of the American law under the new Constitution, and before one could speak of the Constitution, one had to be
drawn to the principles of general jurisprudence. But before that, as
Wilson said, we had to be drawn back to "the philosophy of mind"—
to the principles of understanding themselves, built into the nature
of the human person. Wilson took the occasion to point out that the
law in America would be planted on an entirely different ground
from that of the law in England. That law in England, made familiar
by Blackstone, began in the style of legal positivism with the notion
of a sovereign issuing commands. But the law in America, he wrote,
would begin "with another principle, very different in its nature and
operations":

> [L]aws derived from the pure source of equality and justice must be
> founded on the consent of those, whose obedience they require. The
> sovereign, when traced to his source, must be found in the *man*.[8]

The law began, that is, not with the power of a sovereign issuing
commands, but with the notion of a man, a human being, a moral
agent, tendering his consent. But once again, this whole construction
had to begin, as John Paul II would say, with the most emphatic understanding of the human person: that being who formed the subject
and object of the law. To speak of rendering consent is to speak of a
creature capable of weighing reasons, making a promise, and grasping an obligation to respect that promise, along with the laws he has
helped to make.

But when we say those things we find ourselves stating again the
central truth proclaimed in the Declaration of Independence, or that
"proposition," as Lincoln put it, on which the republic was founded:
"all men are created equal." That was, as Lincoln said, "the father of
all moral principle" among us. It did not proclaim that people were
equal in all respects—that they were equally intelligent or beautiful
or equally virtuous and deserving. The law is not obliged to treat the

8. *Chisholm v. Georgia*, 2 Dallas 419, at 458.

innocent and the guilty in the same way, but to judge each person by the same standard. What the proposition meant was that beings who could give and understand reasons over matters of right and wrong deserved to be ruled with the rendering of reasons, in a government that elicited their consent. In his speech at the Cooper Union in 1860, Lincoln had remarked on those black slaves who had not thrown in with John Brown at Harper's Ferry. Even in their ignorance, as Lincoln said, they could see that the schemes of this white man would not conduce to their well-being.[9] In other words, they might have been unlettered, but they were beings capable of deliberating about the conditions of their well-being, and they did not deserve to be annexed to the purposes of other men without their consent. Or to put it another way, before they were annexed or committed to the projects of others, they deserved to have reasons given to them.

Lincoln said that anyone who would try to remove a government by consent would have to strike at that central "truth" of the Declaration, and that would be, as he said, "one hard nut to crack." It would also be a warning sign, setting off the alarms and whistles. We have now seasons of experience to bear out Lincoln's sense of things, and we might put the matter in this way: when critics or skeptics or cynics start sneering at the truth of the Declaration, they will find themselves attacking two things. They will deny that we can have a rational knowledge of moral truths—of the things that are just or unjust, right or wrong—and in denying that we can indeed give and understand reasons over matters of right and wrong, they will be denying in effect the distinctive nature of human beings, the nature that forms the ground of natural, or human, rights. They would deny, in short, what John Paul II calls the truth about the human person. What I want to lay before you is a series of examples of the forms that this denial may take, forms that have become quite familiar to people who stand

9. See Lincoln, Address at the Cooper Union (February 27, 1860), in *The Collected Works of Abraham Lincoln,* ed. Roy P. Basler (New Brunswick, N.J.: Rutgers University Press, 1953), vol. 3, pp. 539–41.

in what we used to call the circles of the educated. They are different forms in which people with pricey educations have talked themselves out of a confidence in reason itself, and without quite realizing it, talked themselves out of the notion that there is indeed a distinct nature, which forms the ground of judgment about the things that are truly right or wrong for human beings.

If we begin simply with that celebrated truth of the Declaration, we could hardly offer a more notable example than that of the famous historian Carl Becker and his highly praised book, *The Declaration of Independence,* from 1922. Becker dealt with the politics of the Declaration and the shifts in the successive drafts, but on the central meaning of the Declaration he affected a stand of agnosticism. "To ask whether the natural rights philosophy of the Declaration of Independence is true or false," he said, "is essentially a meaningless question."[10] It was a meaningless question because, as a moral question, it could not be the object of answers that could be judged true or false, especially by a historian, for the modern historian now understood that knowledge, including moral knowledge, was historically bound. We could understand things only within our historical epoch. And after Darwin we were no longer under the superstition of supposing that there was a fixed human nature that remains the same, and moral truths that retain their truths in all times and places.

But then, almost twenty years later, in the summer of 1941, Hitler turned on Stalin and launched the invasion of Russia. France had fallen and for all of those with eyes to see it was apparent that if Hitler knocked out Russia, the game, so to speak, would be over. At that moment, Alfred Knopf thought it was time to issue a new edition of Becker's book on the Declaration of Independence, with a new foreword. And in that foreword Becker could write that the only hope for the West at this moment was that men could still be moved to risk their lives for those lofty sentiments in the Declaration of Indepen-

10. Carl Becker, *The Declaration of Independence* (New York: Alfred Knopf, 1942; originally published in 1922), p. 277.

dence—those lofty sentiments that we knew, however, were not true!

Becker acknowledged at least that there was this enduring or, as he called it, this "immemorial" question of human liberty—to which Harry Jaffa responded with a talmudic question: if there is an immemorial question of human liberty, is it not plausible then that there is an immemorial principle of human liberty.[11] But if that were the case, that "principle" would find its origin in a nature of human beings, a capacity to deliberate about the uses of personal liberty, and the question figures to persist only if that nature of human beings in fact endures across the epochs.

Let me take another reflection of the same problem, from our day, just to suggest that the same fallacy seems remarkably to endure across the years for the historians, even if they do not think that the nature of man endures. I offer as a brief but telling example Professor James McPherson's *What They Fought For,* a book that drew on the moving, literate letters written home by soldiers on both sides of the Civil War. Contrary to the conventional line that soldiers fight for their fellows or their comrades, rather than the cause, McPherson finds the most compelling record in these letters that these ordinary men had the clearest sense of those moral and political ends for which they were willing to risk their lives. McPherson records a kind of electric current that ran through the North and the Union forces when Lincoln issued the Emancipation Proclamation. As limited as that measure was, everyone understood that it reflected a moral condemnation of slavery, and with that move, understood in that way, the cause of the Union seemed to be lifted onto another plane. McPherson clearly locates himself on that plane; his own preferences run to the Union side. But that is all he can claim. For he offers a comparable respect for those people who were willing to fight to the death to defend a way of life that encompassed human slavery. After all, as he

11. See Harry Jaffa in his magisterial, long-awaited sequel to *Crisis of the House Divided* (1959), his further meditations on the speeches and statecraft of Abraham Lincoln, *A New Birth of Freedom* (Lanham, Md.: Rowman & Littlefield, 2000), p. 99.

put it, they were willing to die for their beliefs.[12] But that is precisely the stance of the historians, who will not claim to cast a judgment on moral things. All they will do, in the style of social scientists, is record the fact that people believed these propositions about their cause or held to those beliefs with a certain intensity. Yet of course, we would not measure the rightness of any cause by the willingness of zealots, or true believers, to die in its service. In the aftermath of the bombing of the World Trade Center, we would probably find even professors reluctant now to credit the moral plausibility of a cause simply on the fact that the believers were willing to die for it. But that stance has indeed become the guiding principle for many academics and historians precisely as confidence has receded that they had, available to them, reasoned grounds of judgments on the rights and wrongs done in other places and other times.

But that moral confusion leads the historian, as the social scientist, to give a false account. It should be plain that the Union soldiers recalled by McPherson were not at all willing to credit the possibility that the cause of the Confederacy was quite as plausible as their own because the Southern soldiers were willing to die for it. If that were the case, they would have had to assume that they themselves were willing to give up their lives in a cause that had no evident justification. In order to absorb McPherson's understanding, these Union soldiers would have had to entertain the possibility that they might have

12. James M. McPherson, *What They Fought For, 1861–65* (New York: Anchor Books, 1994), p. 34. McPherson quoted some rather precise, moving passages, from soldiers who evidently understood a connection between the Union and the cause of personal freedom. "[T]hese words," he notes, "occurred in letters to loved ones from men on the front lines who did give their lives. They must be taken seriously." Still later: "These words were not mawkish melodrama; [these men] meant what they said." They meant what they said—they had a claim to be taken seriously—because the sentiments they expressed accounted for their willingness to risk their lives in the cause. But of course that is a measure that would have been satisfied by the terrorists of September 11. And it is by that measure that McPherson could treat with a comparable respect the devotion of the soldiers on both sides in the Civil War.

been wrong in their devotion to the Union: they had to be willing, that is, to have the gravest doubts about the connection they made between the Union and a government by consent, the connection that Lincoln made the center of his teaching; or in their rejection of slavery in principle. Unless they could earnestly have affected doubt on these things, they could not have exemplified the understanding of McPherson as he gave this account of them and their counterparts on the other side, the men who were evidently willing to die for their own version of the republic with slavery. But that is to say, McPherson cannot understand these Union soldiers *as they understood themselves.* He must evidently think that they were wrong in their conviction that their position was underlain by a truth about the human person; and if they were so fundamentally mistaken—so willing to lose their lives, and take the lives of others, in the name of a false cause—why should they be the objects of such respect or veneration on his part? In short, the perspective of the modern historian makes him singularly incapable of explaining, as the title goes, *What They Fought For.*

This problem would seem to be endemic in the work of modern historians, and yet it would seem to be at odds with the rudiments of what we would understand as a social science. It was no one other that Max Weber who insisted to us that social science must be able to explain the nature of any act from within—in the sense of explaining how the actor himself understood what he was doing. Aristotle remarked at one point in the *Ethics* that a man could be committing adultery, in effect, without knowing that the woman was married, and so we could not impute to him an intention or even willingness to engage in adulterous acts. And with moral judgment, we must be especially attentive to the point that a description of the gross behavioral act is not a sufficient ground on which to form a moral judgment. We may be told that Jones goes to the garage of Smith and takes the hose on the wall, and yet we would not have learned enough just yet to say that we had just described a "theft." Jones might have had permission to borrow the hose. Or, there might have been a fire in the house, and

Jones grabbed the hose with the intention to putting it back later. We would say, in ordinary language, that Jones was "justified" in his act even though he hadn't secured permission. Either way, we would not have a theft. The lesson, again, is that, before we cast a moral judgment, we must understand the intentions, or the reasons, that animated the actor.

Beyond that, we know that conduct that is, for all we can see, the same, may spring from maxims, or reasons, that are strikingly different. And so suppose we are told that two owners of restaurants in my town of Amherst, Massachusetts, both decide that they will not discriminate on the basis of race in admitting customers to their establishments. Owner A reached his conclusion because he understood that race simply cannot "determine" the moral conduct of any person; that from a person's race, therefore, we could not draw any inference as to whether we are dealing with a good man or a bad man, a person who deserves restraint or punishment. Owner B acts in the same way, but makes his way to his judgment through a different path. He thinks it is wise, for business, to accord the rules of his establishment with the ethos that is dominant in the local community. Amherst is a liberal town; and so discrimination would be bad for business.

I used to imagine that both owners were suddenly transported to South Africa in the 1960s or 1970s, when apartheid was still in force. Owner A finds that his position cannot change, since nothing in the grounds or the reasons behind his judgment has been affected by the shift in locale. He knows that the business might not prosper or survive—and he is anything but indifferent to the consequences. Still, he does not know those consequences possibly bear on the validity of the reasons that enjoin him not to draw moral inferences about the worthiness of people on the basis of their race. But Owner B perseveres with his maxim, of honoring the local ethos. When he moves to South Africa, that ethos prescribes racial separation, and to arrange his restaurant in that way is no longer so bad for business. In the example, we would remind ourselves not only that the reasons matter, profoundly, but that some reasons are virtually indifferent to shifts in locale and to the prospect of unpleasant consequences.

Now I bother to go into some detail in mentioning these things because it has struck me recently that these understandings will often separate the philosopher from the lawyer, and it is not clear that, in this respect, the lawyer is more anchored in the world. What brought this home to me is a case that has been a concern of mine for a long while: *Floyd v. Anders*, in 1977. A child had actually survived an abortion, for twenty days, and a surgery, before he died. The question was posed as to whether there had been an obligation to preserve his life, and the answer, tendered by Judge Clement Haynsworth, was no. As Haynsworth "explained," the mother had decided on abortion, and therefore, "the fetus in this case was not a person whose life state law could protect."[13] That was not a "child"; it was a "fetus" marked for "termination." To put it another way, the right to an abortion meant the right to an "effective abortion" or a dead child. That notable case lay behind the proposal that I've been identified with over the years, the proposal to begin legislating on abortion by proposing simply to protect the child who survived the abortion. That proposal has since become the Born-Alive Infants Protection Act. For years, however, that measure was resisted among the pro-life leadership because it was thought to be altogether too moderate. The skeptics seemed not to grasp the point that the purpose of the legislation was to plant premises in the law—to say, for example, that it made no sense to pass a law of this kind unless we understood that the child who survived the abortion had a claim to the protection of the law; a claim that did not pivot on the question of whether anyone happened to *want* her. One pro-life lawyer simply could not see that point because he did not see that the courts took seriously the claim to an "effective abortion," in killing the child born alive. He would point out to me that this case of *Floyd v. Anders* never got anywhere, never gave rise to any

13. *Floyd v. Anders*, 444 F.Supp. 535, at 539 (1977).

ruling from the Supreme Court. In one case, *Planned Parenthood v. Ashcroft*, in 1983, Justice Powell had noted a doctor making the claim that the right to an abortion had to entail the right to an "effective abortion" or a dead child. And Powell pronounced that argument "remarkable."[14] From that comment, the lawyer was inclined to draw the inference that the Supreme Court would never credit that argument, and that any bill on the subject was essentially beside the point. But as I pointed out, to say that an argument was "remarkable" was not the same as saying that it was "wrong," and still less was it to explain the ground of its wrongness.

What we proposed to do was make the argument explicit, and invite people on the other side—the partisans of abortion—to join us or repudiate our claim. Our own claim, honestly proclaimed, was that if they gave us that premise we would roll back their defense of abortion, step by step. And after all, if the right to an abortion is predicated on the notion that the child counts for nothing—that it has no standing at all when set against the interests of the pregnant woman—then why should a woman's right be impaired merely because the child happened to come out alive? Sure enough, when we finally came forth with that proposal as a serious legislative measure, in the summer of the year 2000, and we scheduled hearings, the National Abortion Rights Action League (NARAL) actually came out in opposition to that measure. They opposed, that is, a measure to protect a child born alive. To their credit, they were more sensitive to the issue in principle than many pro-life congressmen, for they realized that they could not recognize the standing of the child in this way, as an entity receiving the protections of the law, without putting in place premises that would unravel their whole position.

In July 2000, just six days after the hearings on the Born-Alive Infants Protection Act, a federal court in New Jersey struck down that state's version of the law on partial-birth abortion. This decision

14. See *Planned Parenthood v. Ashcroft*, 462 U.S. 476, at 485, n. 7.

came just a few weeks after the Supreme Court, in *Stenberg v. Carhart,* struck down the law on partial-birth abortion in Nebraska, and by inference, in thirty other states. The federal court of appeals in the Third Circuit drew that inference for the law in New Jersey, but Judge Maryanne Trump Barry made it clear that she would have reached the same result even if the Supreme Court had not given precise guidance in the Stenberg case. Judge Barry was offended at the pretension of the legislators to draw a distinction that hinged upon the delivery of a child at the point of birth. The claim of the legislators was that, at the point of delivery, the pregnancy had ended, and the right to end a pregnancy should not control the events taking place here, the killing of a child at the point of delivery. Judge Barry expressed her contempt for the effort to draw such a line between the child in the womb and the child at the point of birth. That distinction has been known to common sense for millennia, but the application of that distinction in these cases, she thought, involved "semantic machinations, irrational line-drawing, and an obvious attempt to inflame public opinion":

> the Legislature would have us accept, and the public believe, that during a "partial-birth abortion" the fetus is in the process of being "born" at the time of its demise. It is not. A woman seeking an abortion is plainly not seeking to give birth.[15]

This opinion must surely stand as the marker for the emergence of a kind of postmodernist jurisprudence. For the argument now was that it was all, in the end, a matter of perceptions, of "semantics" and "line-drawing": there were no objective facts—no birth, no "child" being killed at the point of birth, because the mother, after all, had elected an abortion. Once she had made that fateful choice, there was no child to be killed, no birth to take place. For as Judge Barry said, the pregnant woman was "plainly not seeking to give birth." What the judge "saw" in the case would depend entirely on the theories she was willing to install. But it also confirmed what even many pro-life law-

---

15. *Planned Parenthood v. Farmer,* 220 F.3d 127, at 143 (July 26, 2000).

yers had refused to believe: Judge Haynsworth's opinion in *Floyd v. Anders* was not an anomaly or an aberration; it was being established as the reigning orthodoxy now among many federal judges.

NARAL was being quite sensitive to the question in principle, and acting very much in character, when it made the decision to oppose this most modest move of ours to protect the child who survived the abortion. But Congressman Jerry Nadler, from Greenwich Village, thought that they were exposing themselves and the Democratic Party to serious embarrassment if they insisted that their allies in Congress vote against the bill to protect the child born alive. And so Nadler gave them in effect this counsel: play rope-a-dope, go with the punch, do not oppose this bill. It is very modest, it will make but the smallest change, and NARAL would create more trouble for itself if it opposed the bill, and compelled its allies among the Democrats to argue against it. For that willingness to express their real views would indeed give us the kind of argument and debate we were seeking, the kind of debate that would draw attention to the bill and make its meaning all the clearer. With that counsel, offered by Nadler and accepted by NARAL, the bill sailed through its markup in the Committee on the Judiciary by a vote of 22 to 1, and it was headed to the floor.

It was apparent to us, the drafters and managers of the bill, that the other side was afraid to vote against it, and it was seeking to counter the bill by treating it as a matter of little significance. Our response was to raise the level of tension through the simplest and most transparent device of all—which was to make more explicit the reasons, or principles, behind the bill. I had suggested to the chairman of the subcommittee on the Constitution, Charles Canady, that we return to Felix Frankfurter's plea that legislation contain again preambles, which can set forth their premises and their purposes. In this case, it was too late for a preamble, but we could supply the "findings" that supported the bill. That is, the bill was, after all, modest; its purpose was to teach and plant premises in the law. And so now, we suggested, let us draw the lines more sharply—and draw out the other side—by making those premises explicit. As part of the findings, we would repudiate the claim that the right to an abortion is the right to an effective abortion or a dead child. But as we sought to explain the premises, we could earnestly say to the other side, If we don't have this right, correct it. Amend the findings. But as far as we can see, it didn't seem coherent to vote for this measure unless one understood propositions of this kind: that the child had a claim to the protection of the law, a claim that did not pivot on whether anyone happened to "want" her. But that suggested in turn that the child had an intrinsic dignity, which commanded our respect and the protection of the law; and in that case, the dignity of the child could not be *contingent* on her location, or whether she served the interest of anyone else.

Now, did we have those things wrong? Would we say, rather, that we protect the child because it somehow pleases us to protect her—and that as soon as it ceases to please us, we would cease to protect her? If so, we ought to make that point explicit. Or if that is what the defenders of abortion truly would say, when pushed to give their reasons, they should be compelled to face that fact, to look plainly at the reasons that come along with their position.

What can be reported, at least, is that our sense of things was confirmed. The announcement of those findings, attached to the bill, did indeed raise the level of tension—which showed that it did make the most profound difference politically when the reasons were made explicit. What we had not counted on, however, was that the explosion would come, not among the Democrats, but among the Republicans. The vote on the bill was scheduled for September 26, 2000, but on the morning of the vote a group of so-called "moderate" Republicans demanded a meeting with the Republican leadership of the House over the matter of the Born-Alive bill. Of course, only within the jargon of the American media would people be labeled "moderates" when they refused to contemplate the restriction of even a single abortion out of an annual volume of 1.3 million. What those so-called "moderates" threatened now, to their leadership, was the prospect of join-

ing with the Democrats in adjourning the House if the managers really went to the floor with those "inflammatory" findings. This was
in the fall, just as the presidential campaign was heating up. And this
threat came from the same Republicans who had bent themselves out
of shape, virtually giving in to Bill Clinton on every spending bill, lest
they give the president a pretext for closing down the government yet
again, and yet again saddling them with the blame.

Charles Canady, called into the meeting, could hardly believe the
conversation. As he recalled later, he found himself wondering whether his colleagues really thought that there was a powerful constituen-
cy in their districts who would be moved to a spasm of retaliation if
it looked as though their congressman were too ardently opposed to
infanticide. He was not prepared then for what happened next: Henry
Hyde, of all people, leaned in, acting as the statesman, and pulled the
rug out from under him. Hyde was the chairman of the full Judiciary
Committee, and very much a team player. In that spirit, Hyde made
the decision to pull the findings, and go to the floor without them.
Hyde was a seasoned pro-lifer, but he reasoned in this way: he could
preserve a House under the direction of pro-lifers—with pro-lifers
in charge of the Judiciary Committee—only if the party could hold
a Republican House. Holding Republican control in a House closely
divided meant going to the aid even of Republicans who were "pro-
choice" or even adamantly pro-abortion, if those Republicans found
themselves hanging by only a thread of a lead in a marginal district.

Still, it was a matter of practical judgment: was it really necessary
to gut the section that accomplished the purpose of the bill—the section that would dramatize to the public the premises that shaped the
current laws on abortion; the premises that were being challenged
now in the bill? We thought not, but in any event, the bill went to the
floor in that way, and it sailed through with a vote of 380 to 15. Too
large a vote. To change the figure, when an item clears a market so
quickly, that may be a sign that the good is underpriced. And yet the
dropping of the findings did not buy good will from the pro-choice,

or pro-abortion, people. They were furious at us, and Jerry Nadler de-
nounced us for a "dishonest" bill meant to provide a "trap" for the defenders of abortion. And yet, how dishonest? We had been clear from
the beginning in our presentation of the bill and what we hoped to accomplish, in starting a movement that would go step by step, extend-
ing the protections of the law for unborn children. I raise the matter
to bring out a connection again to my main theme: I would suggest
that the real dissimulation here attached to those people who voted
for the bill out of cynicism, even when they could not possibly share
any of the premises, or reasons, that make the bill coherent.

I will not regale you with the account of this bill since then, but
note that we were astonished when Mr. Bush never endorsed it, or
sought to make use of the bill during his campaign. For that reason
perhaps the bill never made it to the floor of the Senate. It died with
the Congress and it had to be renewed in the current Congress. The
bill was introduced by Charles Canady's successor as the chairman
of the subcommittee on the Constitution, Steve Chabot of Ohio. He
managed to attract a small army of co-sponsors, including people like
Sue Myrick of North Carolina. But this time the findings were placed
there in the beginning by the staff, and arranged even more artfully to
unfold an argument as they advanced. What is more, those findings
elicited the full support and enthusiasm of the sponsors—and of the
Republican leadership. But then another surprise: the findings were
thrown out, waved aside, with a flick of the wrist, by Henry Hyde's
successor as chairman of the Judiciary Committee, James Sensenbrenner of Wisconsin. Sensenbrenner had the reputation of a tough
conservative and pro-lifer—but then what happened? The word was
that Sensenbrenner did not wish to appear to be a less effective chairman than Henry Hyde. Hyde had brought in the bill with a vote of
380 to 15, and Sensenbrenner did not want to appear to preside over
an erosion of support. Without question, there would have been an
erosion of votes if the findings, or the reasons, had been made explicit, and if there ensued the kind of debate and resistance we surely

would have encountered. But we did not need the box score, with the outsized vote. What we wanted was the debate: we wanted the proponents of abortion to face up to their reasons, and in fact suffer the embarrassment of having to acknowledge those reasons as their own. And we could not see why the Republican leadership should take it as part of its responsibility to help the Democrats and the partisans of abortion to avoid that embarrassment, *by avoiding any need to lay out the reasons behind their position.*

It should be plain that this turn of events cannot be ascribed to any interest on the part of James Sensenbrenner and others in making life easier for the Democrats. These moves can be explained, I think, finally only in this way: that, for many congressmen and politicians, including politicians who claim to be conservative and pro-life, "reasons" just do not seem all that important. Or they see no connection between politics and the business of giving reasons—as though it makes no difference, creates no strains or embarrassments, as people are compelled to face the conflicts with their allies or the inconsistencies in their own arguments. Or, that it makes not the slightest practical difference if people are compelled to face their own premises, the premises that dare not speak their name in public.

Felix Frankfurter once remarked, in exasperation over his colleagues, that we are not kadis, sitting under a tree, dispensing judgments without any concern for the reasons that support those judgments. For as Frankfurter understood, those reasons suggest the rules that we think define the condition of justice; the rules we expect to follow then presumptively in similar cases that arise in the future. And yet, we are now finding some accomplished jurists who affect a new kind of sophistication, and insist to us that giving reasons in that way, or reconciling decisions with the precedents of the past, should not be considered so decisively important. That argument has been offered, quite notably recently by one of the most visible jurists in the country, Judge Richard Posner, of the federal court of appeals in the Seventh Circuit. Posner cut a considerable figure in the academy, at the University of Chicago, as part of the movement of law and economics, and in that posture he has been dismissive, to the point of contempt, of the contributions of moral philosophy to the law. He has offered a species of libertarianism, mingled with a rather unalloyed version of utilitarianism, and in that vein he has sought to make an argument of late for a style of "pragmatism" on the part of judges. As Stanton Evans used to say, the problem with pragmatism is that it doesn't work. Which is to say, it soon reveals all of the problems that strain the coherence of any utilitarian perspective. But in that style Posner has argued in his book *The Problematics of Moral and Legal Theory*[16] that "pragmatist judges" should "always try to do the best they can do for the present and the future, unchecked by any felt *duty* to secure consistency in principle with what other officials have done in the past."[17] To put it mildly, he would not burden judges with an obligation "to find the result in the present case that would promote or cohere with the best interpretation of the legal background as a whole." The pragmatist judge, he says, has "different priorities": "He wants to come up with the decision that will be the best with regard to future and present needs."[18]

Mark Twain famously said of Wagner's music that it wasn't as bad as it sounded; and I'm tempted to think that Posner may be converting a familiar and plausible stance into something needlessly unsettling. Thoughtful jurists in the past have encountered cases where the precedents have not been persuasive, or those precedents would not render justice in the case at hand. The judges have sought then to reflect anew about a more satisfying ground in principle for their judgment. In other cases, judges, no less than political men, may find the need to act with prudence, and hold back from applying a principle in a mechanistic way, when it may be inapt.[19]

16. Cambridge, Mass.: Harvard University Press, 1999.
17. Ibid., at p. 241; italics in original.
18. Ibid., at p. 242.
19. As a case in point, I have argued in print for years on abortion, and I've sought

But that kind of move could be understood in a more classic vein as the exercise of prudence. It is not a matter of winging it from one case to another, looking for a desirable outcome, or an outcome with an imbalance of utility over costs. The traditional approach tries to get clear on the principles that can finally justify a judgment, but then show some practical wisdom, or prudence, in applying the rules from one case to another. There is no need then for Posner to impose a scheme of utilitarianism, unchecked by any of those niggling concerns for the principled ground of the judgment. What I would pick out here, however, as a special concern is the way in which Posner could proclaim, with such a flourish, that there should be no "duty" to reconcile our judgments with the decisions that were handed down in the past. That obligation could be waved aside so cavalierly only if one forgets the deepest principle from which that obligation springs. Let me work my way back, taking a notable recent case of legal and moral judgment that readily admits a judgment based on utility. I offer, for the point at hand, the impeachment of William Jefferson Clinton.

In his own book on the impeachment, Judge Posner recognized that the charges against Clinton, for the obstruction of justice in the case of Paula Jones, were indeed serious charges, not to be dismissed as trivial. Posner considered the judgment on Clinton, though, as a political judgment in the highest sense, involving judgments about the wisdom of removing an elected president. If the matter were regarded simply in a pragmatic way, I suppose that from my own point of view—and the view of many Republicans—there was a rather hefty

---

ways to cut back the holding in *Roe v. Wade*. But my own estimate is that it would not be right now a good thing, overall, if the Court, in one dramatic stroke, overruled *Roe v. Wade*. A move of that kind could set off a reaction of panic, as many people in the country would think that they were about to be dispossessed of something they had come to regard as a fundamental right. The result could be to set off a desperate move to enact *Roe v. Wade* into statutes throughout the land. Far better, in my own estimate, to preserve *Roe v. Wade* as a shell, while steadily scaling it back until one day, with the shortest of steps, it is finally dislodged.

utility in not removing Mr. Clinton. Removing him would have made Al Gore president and put Gore in the position of running for the first time for president as an incumbent already bearing the title. At the same time, Mr. Clinton's presence during the campaign seemed to work as a handicap, or as an enduring source of embarrassment for a political party that continued to hold him up as a model to be esteemed and emulated.

Strictly from a pragmatic view, the Republicans could find less utility in removing Clinton than in keeping him around. And yes, it could be quite unsettling for the country to see an elected president removed. A move of that kind promised to make future removals more likely, in the way that the move to impeach of Richard Nixon set the ground for the impeachment later of Mr. Clinton. And that was precisely the point. I must tell you that, in my own judgment, it was a portentous thing, almost thirty years ago, a critical undermining of the separation of powers, when a president of the United States was brought under the compulsory powers of a court to surrender his personal papers and tapes, and forgo any claim of privilege attaching to the conversations he had with people in his own office. A president is not above the law, but there are serious questions about the distribution of power when a president is put under the control of an unelected judge. In my own estimate, also, there are some serious questions engaged in the problem of a president being drawn into a courtroom as a defendant during the term of his presidency. If it were left to me, then, Mr. Clinton would not have been drawn into a trial on the question of whether he had subjected Ms. Paula Jones to a kind of sexual harassment. But the critical thresholds had been crossed years ago with Mr. Nixon. The barriers of executive privilege had been swept away. The president's immunity from being summoned into a court, to answer charges, seems to have been dissolved. I would add that it was not my own political friends who had brought forth new federal laws and regulations dealing with sexual harassment. It was the liberal side of our national political family who insisted that this sort of offense was serious enough to merit trials in a federal forum. American liberals had brought forth these laws, with moral conviction, and they had swept away the main barriers that would have sheltered a president from the prospect of being drawn into the courtroom in the case of Paula Jones. And so the question now was whether the people who had brought forth those laws, and set in place the precedents for the impeachment of Mr. Nixon, were willing to live themselves under the laws they had legislated for others.

I do not say that those laws were indefensible at all points, but they have their problematic qualities, and it could be that, when faced with the implications of enforcing them, we may find reasons to think again, and possibly repeal them. But we cannot get to that point of reflecting seriously on matter unless we are willing to begin with a willingness to respect the precedents of the past as a critical part of living under the laws we would lay down for others. I would point out that this seems precisely what has taken place in regard to the statute on independent counsels. The Democrats brought forth that statute in the days following Watergate to deal with the kind of problem posed by the firing of Archibald Cox as the special prosecutor. Since those days, the law has been used mainly against the members of Republican administrations, and defended most vigorously by the Democrats. But when even a fastidious lawyer like Ken Starr set to work under that statute in the investigation of President Clinton, Democrats began to acquire the deepest revulsion for a statute, and for an apparatus of prosecution, that they had once defended with a deep passion.

But on the matter of impeachment, William Bennett and I posed the spare question in a piece in the *Wall Street Journal.* We recalled that articles of impeachment had been voted in regard to Richard Nixon on the basis of serious charges that he had committed perjury, that he had suborned or encouraged the perjury of others, and in that way, contributed to an obstruction of justice. Now, without claiming to judge just yet whether Mr. Clinton had been guilty of those same offenses, the question we put was, Were the same standards, the same legal rules, to be applied to Mr. Clinton?[20]

When Judge Posner raises a serious doubt that the judges, or officers of the law, should understand a *duty* to reconcile their judgments with the judgments handed down in the past, he seems to be loosening his hold on the moral core of the rule of law, but without the sense that there is anything especially significant taking place. Perhaps the matter would be clearer from another direction if we recalled that passage in John Locke, in the *Second Treatise*, where Locke really pierced to the core of what we have come to understand as the separation of powers. Locke wrote:

> And because it may be too great a temptation to human frailty, apt to grasp at power, for the same persons who have the power of making laws, to have also in their hands the power to execute them . . . [I]n well-ordered commonwealths, where the good of the whole is so considered as it ought, the legislative power is put into the hands of divers persons who, . . . have by themselves, or jointly with others, a power to make laws, which when they have done, being separated again, they are themselves subject to the law they have made; which is a new and near tie upon them to take care that they make them for the public good.[21]

To put it another way, the structure of the separation of powers works to impart this caution—and this mandate—to those who legislate: you had better be careful in the laws you frame because you will not be given the right to direct prosecutions under those laws. Once you have passed any bill into a law, that law will be put in hands other than your own to administer—and those could be unfriendly hands, the hands of people who count themselves as your political enemies. Therefore, as a matter of high prudence, you should be careful not to legislate for others what you would not be willing to see applied, with

20. Our piece ran under the title "Politicians Need to Ask Voters Some Tough Questions," *Wall Street Journal* (October 13, 1998), p. A22.

21. Locke, *Second Treatise on Civil Government,* Sec. 143.

its full force, against yourself. But that is to say, the point about the separation of powers is that it is a way of rendering operational the very logic of a moral principle, the logic of the categorical imperative or what some philosophers would call the universalizability principle: are you acting now to advance your own interests, or are you acting on a maxim that is fit to be installed as a universal law?

Of course, it may be that if Judge Posner is pragmatic or utilitarian, there is no particular force that attaches to the logic of a moral principle. Whether it is indeed right or valid to respect the laws we lay down for others may be, in this construction, quite beside the point. For the question may be: will the society be better off, by and large, in the long run, if people act in a principled way, or might it be more peaceful or salutary under certain cases to avoid that business of applying our principles to the vexing case at hand? But as I have remarked, that kind of understanding could have been encompassed by the classic tradition of prudence, with this difference: that we would begin with an awareness of the principles that claim our respect, and we would carry the burden of justification when we would depart from them. When we begin, though, with a willingness to do what seems to have use or utility for us, there may be a hidden premise there that is quite unlovely. In the case of Judge Posner, that hidden premise might have revealed itself in the litigation over partial-birth abortion, where Posner voted at every opportunity to strike down the law presented to him, from the State of Wisconsin, and express a certain contempt for the moral understanding that animated those laws. In *Planned Parenthood v. Doyle,* he acknowledged that "partial-birth abortion is a gruesome procedure." But he went on to observe that "all abortion procedures, and indeed a vast number of surgical procedures unrelated to the reproductive process, including forms of cosmetic surgery that strike many people as frivolous, are bloody and horrible."[22] In the style of postmodernism, abortion was removed

22. 162 F 3d 463, U.S. Court of Appeals, Seventh Circuit (November 3, 1998), at 470.

from the domain of truth to the domain of appearance: some people were revolted by abortions, some were revolted by face-lifts and nose-bobs. All of these procedures are bloody, they remove tissues, they make people queasy—and some of them simply involve the dismembering of a live, innocent human being. But in this way, the killing of a child (or a "fetus") is placed on the same plane as a nose-bob.

Posner had shot to fame as an adept in the field of law and economics, which sought to use the most rigorous methods of statistics in weighing the validity of propositions or theories. And yet the curious thing, which one cannot help but notice, is that those high powers of analysis have never been brought to bear on the elementary question here: on what grounds of evidence or principle would the child in the womb be regarded as anything less than a human being, whose injuries then counted—whose injuries had some standing in the eyes of the law? In the case of partial-birth abortion, Posner had never sought to measure or compare the harm done to the mother as opposed to the irreparable harm done to the child, whose skull was being crushed. That formidable apparatus of social scientific inquiry, all the acuteness of economic analysis and the calculus of utility, never seemed to come into play. Oddly enough, the concern for utility was simply trumped, overcome, by a kind of axiom: Posner simply took it as a given that the pregnant woman was, in this situation, the sole bearer of rights. Her interests, or her own calculations of the things that were undesirable, had to be taken as decisive. And because the problem was cast in that way, the unborn child simply did not count; it had no standing. The unlovely premise, as I said, whose presence we suspect is this: when people offer theories of utilitarianism or pragmatism, they still must begin with a sense of the persons, those human persons, we might say, whose interests count, whose injuries are to be weighed in the balance as we weigh utility. The libertarians and utilitarians, for all of their sympathies proclaimed for the liberties of ordinary people, still find themselves backing to the premise of the Rule of the Strong. We have in abortion two lives, but the one who was here earlier, the one who is more visible, the one who has the power to kill the other, is the one who truly matters, the one who is indeed sovereign in the weighing of "interests."

What I've been trying to suggest is that these strands are all connected: the reluctance to put in place the reasons behind the judgment; the loss of conviction about applying precedents to cases, the subtle receding from the willingness to honor the precedent and to live by the law handed down earlier, for others; the curious avoidance of bringing reason to bear in testing the very premises of one's policies, especially in explaining why whole classes of human beings have been removed from the class of "persons" and the protections of the law; and finally, the moral drift of backing into the Rule of the Strong, disguised in the most polite of forms, and with language suitably legal.

That point came out sharply, for me, at the law school at Yale a couple of years ago, when I was speaking to the Federalists there. That group draws to itself a contingent of conservative libertarians, and one youngster, of that persuasion, asked with a certain indignation, Why should the pregnant woman be constrained by the law to restrict her own freedom, alter her prospects, abridge or subordinate her interests, for the sake of "this thing" she is carrying? And my response at the time was: we would respect the claims of that unborn child on the same grounds on which we are asked to respect the standing, and the interests, of *that woman* as a moral agent. Tell us the ground on which we accord that respect to her and her interests, and we would claim that precisely the same grounds underlie our concern for the child.

Cardinal Jean-Marie Lustiger touched this question of the libertarians from another angle a few years ago, in the Erasmus Lecture in New York, when he recalled that formula from John Stuart Mill, now made into a common slogan: that our liberty finds its limit at the point at which we start inflicting injuries on others. Lustiger raised the question, Why do those others count? And do they all count? Could we reformulate the matter by saying, "Our liberty finds its limit at those points where we begin to inflict injuries on others *who count*. And we may reserve to ourselves the judgment as to who, exactly, counts." To cast the problem in that way may bring us to the recognition at once that even the traditional formulas of liberalism or libertarianism folded in the assumption that all human beings counted. Even without seeing those others, or weighing their merits, the assumption was that we could not treat them as nothing; that we should have—pardon the expressions—good reasons or justifications when we may injure those others. Which is to say, we have folded into the principles of liberalism the proposition that "all men are created equal." Of course, it would seem to follow then that, if unborn children are among the "others," they should be protected. But it should be equally obvious that the logic of abortion rights has compelled many of our people to talk themselves out of that notion of according equal weight and concern to those unknown others who might be injured by these acts of abortion. And then it might become ever clearer that, with that subtle step, people have talked themselves out of the proposition "all men are created equal," just as they have talked themselves out of the understanding of the human person that comes along with that "proposition," as Lincoln called it.

But affable people with B.A.'s earnestly ask, Can we not simply agree that life is better when people *believe* these things, even if we are not sure that these propositions about the human person are true? And so, at a reunion dinner at Amherst, a member of the Class of '56 came up to ask, Isn't it still possible to study the Founders in the college, and to point up, say, the hypocrisy of Jefferson in proclaiming human equality and yet holding on to his slaves? I responded that yes, it seems always legitimate in the modern academy to point up the hypocrisy of the Founders. But I suggested to him that the discussion is simply purged of its significance if "all men are created equal" is not in fact a truth, a moral truth. For then what would we be saying in deriding Jefferson for his hypocrisy: that he expressed lofty sentiments, yet he continued to hold a form of property that, as far as we know, was defensible, and not wrong? Or would we say that Jefferson was guilty of the offense of being inconsistent? It is hard for people to be consistent in all things, but if there are no grounds for moral truths, what would be the nature of the indictment: that Jefferson had made a mistake, or that he had fallen into an error entirely devoid, however, of moral consequence? If there are no moral truths, why should inconsistency, of all things, amount to a high moral offense?

The person who posed this problem to me was an earnest, public-spirited man, educated to a certain temper, reflective of his age and the currents that were running through the circles of the educated. What he reflected, as I've tried to suggest, is that even affable people, with decent motives and a college education, have fallen into paths, plausible and familiar, that move them away from the sense that there is any importance attached to the discipline of giving reasons or justifications. When they detach themselves from that disposition, they detach themselves also from the understanding that the life of giving reasons is bound up with the justification for political life itself, and with the nature of that creature who alone has the capacity to give and understand reasons over matters of right and wrong. Without quite realizing it, these people detach themselves from the very understanding of "the human person" that underlies this constitutional order and their own *natural* rights.

Aristotle famously remarked that the law is reason freed from all passion.[23] At the heart of the law is the sense of principle—the understanding of right and wrong from which the law emanates when it truly merits the name of law. A political class that has lost the sense that reason matters is a political class that may serve in positions as officers of state, and yet its members will have lost their vocation. At times, the need to clarify the principles entails the need to stage the confrontation or the debate, and that may indeed involve the need to pick a fight. A political class that is persistently reluctant to show that

23. Aristotle, *Politics*, 1287a, in *The Complete Works*, pp. 2042–43.

spirited nature will produce, not merely a politics that is banal, but one that is denatured. In removing the conflict, or removing the argument, one may gently remove as well the moral substance. Aristotle also remarked, in one of his most memorable observations, that if the art were in the material, then ships would be springing, fully crafted, from trees.[24] But ships were not part of the world of "causation," produced through the workings of the laws of nature. Ships were part of a world governed by design, by the awareness of ends, and the shaping of reasons. We may be bringing forth now a political class more and more detached from the sense that there is any particular importance in compelling the other side to come out with their reasons, and claim them as their own. To a political class molding itself in that way, we may not ask only, where is the reason that gives meaning to political life, but where, in all of that, is the *art?* Where do we find the distinctive hand that shows your work? Where do we find the design that marked your understanding, the touch that reflected the experience you had cultivated? And where, finally, do we find the impression, lingering through time, that you were here?

24. "If the ship-building art were in the wood, it would produce the same results by nature." Aristotle, *Physics,* 199b 28, in *The Complete Works,* p. 340.

five

∽

Paul C. Vitz

FROM THE MODERN INDIVIDUAL TO THE

TRANSMODERN PERSON

W^E live, as is well known, at a time when psychology has been extremely influential.[1] Thus, it is not surprising that much of what we understand about the nature of the person has been formed and even understood through the concepts of psychology. It will be useful to describe this influence and to identify the basic dilemmas that psychology has brought to the present understanding of the person. After describing these dilemmas—the problem, so to speak—I will take up the issue of their solution.

1. Early expressions of parts of this paper are in Vitz, "Back to Human Dignity: From Modern to Post-Modern Psychology," *Intercollegiate Review* 31 (1996): pp. 15–23; and "A Christian Theory of Personality," in *Limning the Psyche: Explorations in Christian Psychology,* ed. R. Roberts and M. Talbot (Grand Rapids, Mich.: Eerdmans, 1997), pp. 20–40.

Modern psychology

We begin with what is known as "modern psychology," namely the psychology which began with Sigmund Freud and psychoanalysis and which, I believe, ends with the humanistic or self psychology of Carl Rogers and Abraham Maslow and the cognitive/behavioral psychologists such as Albert Ellis and Aaron Beck. (There are of course many other important psychologists in between.) We will address these and other modern psychologists of importance briefly and then turn to the quite recent postmodern psychology. These two kinds of psychology—modern and postmodern—have created very different kinds of dilemmas concerning the person.

Freud was a product of nineteenth-century secular humanist and Enlightenment thought. For him, the idea of a person or individual was pretty much a given, and the problem was how to explain or interpret the individual from a scientific or semi-scientific perspective. His major emphasis, especially in his early writings, was on the unconscious mind. Our conscious mind, he claimed, was largely under the control of unconscious influences which were rooted in a universal, vaguely biological nature, of sexuality and aggression. Thus, our mental life is largely unconscious, and is understood in psycho-biological terms. There is, of course, a small amount of consciousness, centered in the ego, but for classical psychoanalysis, the ego is a kind of emerging self, a relatively small part of the total psychic structures. Nevertheless, Freud in his own personal and professional life believed strongly in the eventual triumph of rationality in the form of science or reason, both in the life of the culture and in the life of the individual. This was expressed in the goal of psychoanalysis, which was to move toward the conscious life of reason—a goal summarized by the psychoanalytic mantra, "Where id was, ego will be."

After Freud, psychoanalysis developed in two major, interrelated directions. First came what was called "ego psychoanalysis," in which the conscious mind and the ego were given increasing emphasis and increasing power *in* the total psychological economy. This led eventually to the emphasis on separation and individuation as central to the forming of the adult personality or self. By separation, these later psychoanalysts were emphasizing the separation of the infant or child from its mother and the child's subsequent development as an individuated, distinct person. This was a continuation of the previous emphasis on the ego and the conscious mind.

Another group of psychoanalysts, known as object-relations theorists, more or less abandoned the biological, innate, unconscious emphasis of Freud—that is, his (and Melanie Klein's) understanding of the id. Instead, these theorists focused on the first one or two years of life, and concluded that early interpersonal relationships, primarily between the infant and the mother figure, were basic to the formation of the personality. For these psychologists, extremely early internalized persons and relationships represented the nature of the unconscious, but the object-relations theorists also accepted that healthy development meant the increasing freedom of the ego from early unconscious sources of internalized pathology. There was no doubt, for them, that all infants had a similar mental propensity for these relationships. Furthermore, the regularities that they as psychologists were observing represented a roughly universal pattern of human development—and that the strengthening of the conscious ego, sometimes referred to as ego strength, was an important and universal goal.

In summary, then, psychoanalysts generally agree that strengthening ego functions and integrating the psyche and increasing conscious understanding were common positive goals relevant to all. Psychoanalysts might differ about whether the unconscious was primarily biological or the result of very early internalized relationships with others, but they did not disagree about there being a common basis for personhood, and about what the goal of a healthier person might be.

If we turn to the psychology of Carl Jung, we find a similar understanding of the person, even though the particulars are quite different. Jung's unconscious, filled with archetypes, was very different from Freud's. But Jung's unconscious was a collective and universal one; the archetypes were common to all human beings, even though their symbolic expression might later be influenced by the person's particular environment and culture. The goal of Jungian analysis was self-realization, a process described as individuation. Indeed, the self was one of the most important of the universal archetypes. The process of self-realization was brought about through the integration of the archetypes with special emphasis on making them conscious. So, for Jung, the person was this collection of archetypes and the process of integrating around the archetype of the self. And for Jungians, as for Freudians, there was no doubt that the whole system—the self or person—was relatively the same everywhere in its gross anatomy. And again, the goal of this was to make the self more consciously expressed, more integrated, more in charge.

We jump now to the most recent examples of modern psychology, which have also been the most influential here in the United States and are probably more familiar to most Americans than Freudian and Jungian psychology. Both Carl Rogers and Abraham Maslow emphasized the conscious experienced self. That there was such a self they took for granted, and they also took for granted that it was relatively the same everywhere. Both of them emphasized that self-actualization—the constant growing and developing of the self—was the goal of psychotherapy or counseling. Indeed, both of them said that was the goal for life itself. Maslow proposed that the self-actualized person was the ideal person, and Rogers argued that the flowing, developing, self-directed self was the goal for all people. These humanistic or self psychologists were often translated by more popular writers into very influential books which permeated American society. Recall such books as *I'm Okay, You're Okay; Looking Out for Number One*, etc.; this emphasis on the isolated autonomous self doing whatever it wanted in order to actualize itself led in time to various critiques of our increasingly narcissistic society. The cognitive/behavioral psychologists, e.g., Ellis, Beck, also emphasized the conscious mind and the ego or self that took responsibility for cooperating with the therapist and bringing about positive psychological change.

Postmodern psychology

The most effective critiques of the modern understanding of the person or self have come from postmodern theorists. Their critiques identify two major problems. First, they point out that the self is given no definition or systematic foundation in any of these modern psychologies. The self appears to have been always assumed to be self-obvious. It did not occur to the modern theorists that the nature of the self had to be identified and documented. The postmodern critics point out this failure to ground the self in any cogent, independent rationale. Equally important is the postmodern argument that the self is a social construct—that it varies from culture to culture, from historical period to period. That is, these theorists make a case for the relativistic status of the self. The postmodern theorists consider the modern theory of the self a historically and culturally determined phenomenon—a product of the modern West. As a result, there is no natural or universal self, only changing social experiences which today create a kind of weak or incoherent or even arbitrary self.

Let us look in some detail at these interpretations of the self which are postmodernist. Like most writers today, I interpret the postmodern as a form of late modernism: it is modernism using its own inconsistencies to destroy itself. Postmodernism is a kind of "morbid modernism": the "death wish" that was inherent in modernism (e.g., de Sade, Nietzsche) is now leaking out and expressing itself. Thus, as noted, recent postmodern theorists of the self have proposed that the very notion of the autonomous self is incoherent. These theorists are deconstructing the self, and in many ways their critiques signal the beginning of the end of modern psychology.

Kenneth Gergen has provided an influential description of the crisis of the contemporary self by interpreting today's self as "saturated."[2] That is, the variety and complexity of today's styles of living make for a self that is complex, overburdened, and saturated to the point of incoherence. The contemporary American self often lives in two or three different places each year, relates to people in different cities, jobs, and cultures on a regular basis. Meanwhile the media and new technologies flood each person with ever more lifestyles, historical periods, different values, philosophies and religions, hobbies, types of travel, and places to go. Many of these late-modern selves have had two or three marriages, and have extraordinarily complex and unstable family situations. Many of these selves have had two, three, or four different careers. Hence this new saturated self often has several "centers"—it is a polyvalent self. Just keeping up with all this leaves no time for reflection or integration, no time to develop a coherent core to the self. The result is an individual that is so busy responding to immediate, dramatically different situations that no strong, independent self develops. This is what Gergen means by "saturated."

Philip Cushman has gone even further than Gergen: he claims that the modern self or individual is basically empty.[3] Cushman is especially interested in showing that the concept of self is always a reflection of the historical and cultural context—something most psychological theories of the self ignore. In his critique, Cushman expresses a clear postmodernist logic, arguing that the modern, so-called genuine self has always been a kind of illusion. He understands the modern individual, as do most theorists, as a "bounded masterful self that has specific psychological boundaries, an internal locus of control, and a wish to manipulate the external world for its personal ends" (ibid., p. 600).

2. Kenneth Gergen, *The Saturated Self: Dilemmas of Identity in Contemporary Life* (New York: Basic Books, 1991).

3. Philip Cushman, "Why the Self Is Empty," *American Psychologist* 45 (1990): pp. 599–611.

His critique develops along the following lines: Cushman accepts the notion of the traditional self—what is often called the pre-modern self, one that is rooted in family, religious faith, tradition, and community. He accepts these relationships as legitimate, and as central to the traditional self. However, with the rise of modern industrial and technological society, the individual was torn away from these relationships.

Cushman has proposed that the empty self created by the loss of the traditional structures has been filled by two major modern social forces. The first and perhaps most important force is the consumer society, especially its advertising. Thus, today's individual is constructed from the meaning of its purchased products, and from the commercial meaning of our lifestyles. The self is now defined by its automobiles and vacations, by its button-down shirts and barn jackets, even by its brands of beer and perfume. Since we now define the self increasingly through consumption rather than traditional relationships, it is not surprising that the pathologies of our time are narcissism and the inability to maintain long-term commitments to others. Additional media-influenced problems of our day include preoccupation with self-esteem, values confusion, eating disorders, drug abuse, and chronic consumerism.

According to Cushman, the other force which has filled the void at the center of the modern self has been psychology. Psychotherapy, with its search for the origins of personality, with its emphasis on past traumas, on the inner child, on expressing archetypes, and on self-actualization, has constructed the other half of modern identity.

In the late twentieth century, developing some kind of psychological identity—commonly called self-fulfillment—became commonplace. And of course most individuals have turned to popularized forms of psychology to get advice on how to become actualized or fulfilled, and to achieve peace of mind. Advertising strategies have capitalized on this need to glamorize the personality by identifying a particular product with an ideal state of being, the product's "image." Successful ads give the impression that buying the product will free the consumer of personal fears and feelings of inadequacy. The person will introject the product's "image." Thus both psychotherapy and advertising are attempting to relieve the individual's sense of emptiness and to create an individual's identity or self.

Ultimately, of course, Cushman thinks that these modern forces are fundamentally phony, and the self they create is an illusion. He believes that they profoundly fail to satisfy the needs of the self or person in the way that the older relationships once did. As a consequence, Cushman has concluded that the modern self or individual is like a package covered with beautiful wrapping paper—but empty inside.

Perhaps the most extreme position on the contemporary self is proposed by Robert Landy, who has argued that there is no genuine self at all.[4] Landy writes out of a background in theater and has claimed that the contemporary self consists only of roles, as in theatrical roles, which the person chooses. Just as an actor chooses roles, Landy has proposed that the individual consists only of roles, and since they have no coherent center, there is in fact no integrated autonomous self at all. There are, rather, many selves—or really a multi-centered self. Thus, we must let go of what has been thought of as the modern self. Landy admits that letting go of this self goes against scores of philosophers, poets, and theologians who have advocated a core entity that contains the essence of one's being and can be known (ibid., p. 19). The concept of a core self implies that certain behaviors are authentic (the true self) and other behaviors are not (social masks). Inherent in this view is a moral framework wherein rages a battle "between the authentic and god-given forces of light and the inauthentic, demonic forces of darkness" (ibid., p. 19). But this notion of self, however familiar, is—Landy argues—mistaken and must be abandoned. For Landy, the very notion of an authentic self is inau-

4. Robert Landy, *Persona and Performance: The Meaning of Role in Drama, Therapy and Everyday Life* (New York: Guilford, 1993).

thentic. His emphasis on the self as a set of roles has certain similari-
ties to a social self found in some traditional societies. As our culture
becomes more "neo-pagan," it should not be surprising that it returns
to such earlier notions of a less integrated, role-based, multi-centered
self or person.

The postmodern self, in conclusion, is a self which is not integrated, not universal, and in the process of becoming no self at all. For
example, psychologists have recently begun to report hearing clients
complain that the ideal of an integrated, masterful self is too difficult
for them to achieve. It seems like an old, fading heroic vision which
causes a psychological hernia every time they try to achieve it. Hence,
many people today have rejected the older—modern—idea of the integrated self as impossible. The idea of the changing, unstable self—
the new postmodern reality—is expressed in such comments as: "Of
course I promised I would always love you. But that was twenty years
ago, and I am a different person now."

It certainly has been a useful critique that the postmodernists
have developed, for it is true that there was no adequate definition or
theoretical grounding for the modern self. In fact, it looks as though
modern psychology just secularized the older religious notion of the
soul, and gave the issue little further thought. Perhaps we can excuse
Freud and others for failing to lay a clear foundation for the self or
person. After all, as psychologists they proceeded inductively from
observing and thinking about the patient. They and their followers
eventually backed into the issue of a philosophical rationale for their
theories. And although a few modern psychologists, e.g., Fromm, did
talk about personality as affected by culture, the general issue of the
cultural relativity of the self was never addressed.

But the postmodernist position itself is not without serious weaknesses. For example, there is good evidence that a reasonably integrated self is a common, observable, and desirable thing. Take the case of
multiple personality disorder (now called dissociative identity disorder). It is clear that people who have multiple selves, each acting rela-

tively independently of the others, have real trouble with life. In short, this is a pathology which causes great suffering. Healing this condition requires integration of the different selves, under the control of the strongest mature self.[5] So it is clear that extreme emphasis on the relativity and social arbitrariness of the self is a serious overstatement, and this is the central dilemma of the postmodern position—namely how to allow for the stable central character of the self.

A solution: the transmodern person

As an answer to the modern and postmodern problem, let me introduce an alternative understanding of the person which has been emerging recently. I use the term "transmodern" to describe this new vision of the person and perhaps even the new mentality which will follow our present postmodern period. Transmodern means a new understanding which transforms the modern and transcends it. In order to transform modernism it is necessary to be thoroughly familiar with modern ideas, and after going through the "fiery brook," so to speak, to come out on the other side. In addition to transforming modern ideas these transmodern theorists will, I believe, add an important transcendent element to this new understanding. That is, there will be a religious, spiritual, or idealistic aspect central to the transmodern. With respect to the person, the theoretical writers have been primarily theologians and philosophers, but their ideas are directly relevant to psychology, as will be shown there, and in due time these ideas through psychology may strongly affect the culture in general. In part the significance of this approach is due to the fact that these theorists articulate an understanding of the person that is intimately connected with the Judeo-Christian tradition. The first of the preceding modern/postmodern problems for which an answer is giv-

5. See J. E. Davis, "Not Dead Yet: Psychotherapy, Morality and the Question of Identity Dissolution," in *Identity and Social Change,* ed. J. E. Davis (New Brunswick, N.J.: Transaction Publishers, 2000), pp. 158–78.

en by this approach is the problem of a definition and clear theoretical rationale for person or self.

This new rationale—at least new for psychology!—is that the person is brought into existence, or created, by God. It is important here to make clear that the *concept* "person" originated as a special term in the Christian theological debates of the first few centuries. These theologians had the task of defining God as a person, and the Trinity as made up of three persons. The original Latin word "persona" (and its Greek equivalent) referred to the mask worn by a character in ancient theater and sometimes to an individual as citizen, but the development of the notion of person was primarily theological, and Christian. (To the best of my knowledge no psychology text treating the topic of personality has ever acknowledged this deeply Christian religious aspect of the idea of person.)

Now, the concept of God as a person, and human beings as persons created in the image of God, is a fundamental one in the Hebrew Scriptures, which is, of course, where Christian theologians got it. The essential idea is not only that we are a person because we have a physical existence, or body, with a soul or spirit, but also because we are made for relationship, for dialogue, with God—who is a person—and for relationships with others. The relationship is explicitly one of love and involves serious commitment. This foundational idea is summarized in the two great commandments: "Thou shalt love God" and "Thou shalt love thy neighbor as thyself"—principles firmly articulated in the Hebrew Bible.

This means that the essential human motivation and purpose of human life is love. It also means that the barriers to love, such as fear and hatred, become the major psychological problems or sources of pathology. Thus, the goal of life is not lifting repressions, nor is it self-actualization; rather, the goal is love of God and of others. Repressions, sexuality, and inhibitions are not the primary psychological problems; instead, the real issues are fear, anxiety (often caused by loss of love), and the resulting hatreds and angers. No major modern or postmodern psychological theory has put love at the center of personality formation and growth. Nor have they identified hatred, rage, and envy as the major pathologies.

Of course, the first thing God did in creating man was to create us physically. Thus, all of us have an objective physical existence centered in our primate body. This bodily nature is very important and has always been so understood in both the Jewish and the Christian traditions. Since human bodies are all relatively similar (we are one species), this means also that there is a basic human nature rooted in our body and its interactions with external reality. Both modern and postmodern psychologists have greatly neglected the body and in some cases explicitly rejected the notion of any kind of human nature.[6] Today's understanding of the human being, however, developing especially in the fields of neuroscience and biology, is radically challenging both the modern and postmodern view. In the process, this new research is giving scientific support to the theological tradition with its emphasis on the body.[7]

Recently, important philosophical claims for human embodiment have been made by Lakoff and Johnson in *Philosophy in the Flesh: The Embodied Mind and Its Challenge to Western Thought*.[8] These authors, in fact, use much psychological evidence in their case for human embodiment before they go on to develop the body's foundational philosophical significance.

With respect to the embodied self, the beginning of a clear center of the self starts in infancy. In the world of visual experience, the very young child recognizes that it is at the center of the visual world in which it is moving about and which it is observing. It recognizes

6. Freud, as noted, had a vague nineteenth-century biological theory of the mind, but psychoanalysis after Freud has largely neglected the body.

7. For the theological emphasis on the body, see B. Ashley, *Theologies of the Body: Humanist and Christian* (Braintree, Mass.: Pope John Center, 1985); and John Paul II, *The Theology of the Body according to John Paul II: Human Love in the Divine Plan* (Boston: Pauline Books and Media, 1997).

8. New York: Basic Books, 1999.

an invariant center from which it apprehends its grasp of the external physical world. This center of the moving three-dimensional visual world is also a center of awareness or consciousness. This non-verbal centering of the individual is a kind of proto-self. Closely coordinated but distinctively different from the visual center, is a proprioceptive center. The kinesthetic, tactile, and internal cues informing the young child about the location of its body create a similar center of individual consciousness which is unique to each person and again is a kind of proto- and non-verbal self. The visual and proprioceptive centers are of course closely linked; indeed, normally they appear to be merged.[9]

Also from the very beginning of the infant's life there develops an interpersonal understanding of the self. From birth, humans attend closely to the human face and voice, and with the mother-figure begin to develop complex interpersonal interactions like proto-conversations, again, creating a notion of the self as interpersonally defined. By the age of one, if not sooner, language begins developing and the self, based on the understanding of elementary pronouns and possessives (me, mine, you, yours), emerges quickly. This early linguistic self-consciousness has emerged from the earlier bodily interactions and it also includes the biologically based predispositions to language itself.[10]

In addition to the body, the theological-philosophical tradition also focuses on relationships as another foundational property of the person. That is, the God in whose image we are made is explicitly one containing loving relationships in His essence. Specifically, in the Christian emphasis on God as a Trinity, the concept of loving relationship is further developed.

The Protestant theologian T. F. Torrance has done much to illuminate the interpersonal implications of the Trinitarian concept of God in a historical framework.[11] He identified two basic understand-

9. For a summary of these two selves see J. L. Bermùdez, *The Paradox of Self-Consciousness* (Cambridge, Mass.: MIT Press, 1998), chs. 5, 6, and 8.

10. Ibid., pp. 249–65.

11. T. F. Torrance, *The Mediation of Christ* (Grand Rapids, Mich.: Eerdmans, 1983), and *Reality and Scientific Theology* (Edinburgh: Scottish Academic Press, 1985).

ings of God as a person: the first view, the dominant one in Western philosophy, comes from Boethius. The other derives primarily from the patristic period of the Church (especially from the Greek world) and also from the twelfth-century French philosopher and theologian Richard of St. Victor.

Boethius defined a person as "an individual substance of a rational nature." In this concept of "substance" there was a strong emphasis on body and separateness: on what divided one substance from another. The Fathers of the Church and Richard of St. Victor, in contrast, derived their concept of the person from the Holy Trinity. As Torrance noted, Richard defined a person "not in terms of its own independence as self-subsistence, but in terms of its ontic relations to other person, i.e., by a transcendental relation to what is other than it, and in terms of its own unique incommunicable existence."[12] In summarizing Richard's view, Torrance says: "A person is what he is only through relations with other persons" (ibid.).

The contemporary Catholic theologian Joseph Ratzinger, now Pope Benedict XVI, has taken a position strikingly similar to that of Torrance, though the two writers are apparently unaware of each other's thought. Ratzinger wrote:

> Christian thought discovered the kernel of the concept of person, which describes something other and infinitely more than the mere idea of the "individual." Let us listen once again to St. Augustine: "In God there are no accidents, only substance and relation." Therein lies concealed a revolution in man's view of the world: the relation is discovered as an equally valid primordial mode of reality. It becomes possible to surmount what we call today "objectifying thought"; a new plane of being comes into view.[13]

With a Trinitarian emphasis, Ratzinger stated:

---

12. Torrance, *Reality and Scientific Theology*, p. 176.
13. Joseph Ratzinger, *Introduction to Christianity*, translated by J. R. Foster (New York: Herder & Herder, 1970), p. 132.

person must be understood as relation . . . the three persons that exist in God, are in their nature relations. They are, therefore, not substances that stand next to each other, but they are real existing relationships . . . Relation[ship] . . . is not something added to the person, but it is the person itself. In its nature, the person exists only as relation.[14]

The notion of person as relation has implications beyond the theological:

the phenomenon of complete [relatedness], which is, of course, realized in its entirety only in the one who is God . . . indicates the direction of all personal being. The point is thus reached [where] . . . there is a transition from the doctrine of God into . . . anthropology. (Ibid., p. 445)

Ratzinger's use of the term "anthropology" is equivalent to the term "psychology."

Ratzinger seems to imply above that a person is only relation, and by implication that substance is not a necessary component. Elsewhere, however, Ratzinger qualifies this by writing that relation and substance are equally valid primordial modes (or principles) of reality.[15] I also assume that person is both *substance* and *relation*.

Much like Torrance, Ratzinger points out that the definition of "person" by Boethius, as an "individual substance of a rational nature," had unfortunate consequences for Western theology. He recognized that thinking of a person as substance emphasizes the isolated and autonomous notion of person, and that the lack of emphasis on person-as-relation was regrettable. Ratzinger also commented that Richard of St. Victor was an important exception.

Some of the psychological evidence for the importance of relationship in the formation of the person should be noted, however

14. Joseph Ratzinger, "Concerning the Notion of Person in Theology," *Communio* 17 (1990): pp. 439–54 (original German edition, 1973), p. 442.

15. Ratzinger, *Introduction to Christianity*, p. 132.

briefly. Relationships are necessary for normal human existence and development. It is literally true that without ordinary relationships our very substance would cease to exist. A newborn child that has no mothering relationship with another human will die, even if physical needs are met. A person learns to speak through relationships with others, beginning in the first weeks of life, when the infant first listens to its mother's voice. Without relations, a human being does not know language and without language we are hardly human. Certainly there is no reason to think that either an "individual" or a "person" could come into existence who had no relationships with anyone else. This is not to deny the legitimacy of substance. In the present model, substance and relationship are each necessary, but not sufficient determinants of person.

It is important, here, to acknowledge the rich interpersonal understanding of the child developed in the relatively recent psychoanalytic tradition known as object-relations theory. These theorists ignored the body but they did give early relationships their due.

Let's look at this issue from the different perspective proposed by Sampson.[16] He pointed out that "the Western epistemological tradition of Descartes and Kant that marks contemporary cognitive psychology involves an individualistic reduction centered around the 'I think'" (p. 732). In this dominant psychological tradition, "objects are seen to be the products of individual mental operations; the world 'out there' is constituted by the individual's thinking and reasoning processes" (p. 732). Sampson interpreted this as an ideologically biased perspective and he argued that "I think" should in fact be understood as "we think," since our thinking is not just me thinking, it is initially a social construct before it is a private mental event. That is, for Sampson, "we think" comes before "I think."[17] Specifically, Sampson wrote as follows:

16. E. Sampson, "Cognitive Psychology as Ideology," *American Psychologist* 36 (1981): pp. 730–43.

17. Here, Sampson is indebted to L. Vygotsky, *Mind in Society* (Cambridge, Mass.: Harvard University Press, 1978).

... in describing the process of *internalization,* whereby external operations gain an internal representation, Vigotsky notes the key role of other people in a given social and historical context. In his terms, "an interpersonal process is transformed into an intrapersonal process" (Vigotsky, 1978, p. 57). In other words, the basics for the "I think" exist in the prior foundation of the social world; the interpsychological precedes and shapes the intrapsychological.[18]

In addition, the Jewish understanding of themselves as a Chosen People, as a distinctive community, also contains within it a profound sense of the interrelatedness intrinsic to being a person. The interpersonal aspect of Judaism, of each person's relationship to God and to others, has been expressed clearly by Martin Buber in *I and Thou.*[19]

Additional problems with the modern concept of individual

It is clear that, when Carl Rogers entitled his well-known book *On Becoming a Person,*[20] he was simply wrong. What he wrote was a book on becoming an individual, and in particular an autonomous, self-actualizing, independent individual. An individual is created by separating from others, by breaking away, by concentrating psychological thought, energy, and emotion on the self instead of on God and other people.

The founders of modern psychology clearly knew this. The first expression of the ideas that Rogers made more widely known can be found in the earlier writings of Alfred Adler and especially Carl Jung. Adler called his psychology "individual psychology"; Jung called the central process of self-development "individuation." Even the object-

18. Sampson, "Cognitive Psychology," p. 732. For a recent rich discussion that examines the issues of separation, objectivity, and the absence of relationship in the modern period, see C. Gunton, *The One, the Three and the Many* (Cambridge: Cambridge University Press, 1993).

19. Martin Buber, *I and Thou* (New York: Scribner's, 1958; original German edition, 1922).

20. Carl Rogers, *On Becoming a Person* (Boston: Houghton Mifflin, 1961).

relations theorists conceptualized the goal of psychotherapy as freeing one from early internalized interpersonal relationships, often of a pathological kind. They described this as the process of separation and individuation.

Thus, in important respects, what the Judeo-Christian perspective means by person is the opposite of an individual, for a person comes into existence through a body, and by connecting with others, not by separating from them. That is, much of modern psychology, especially humanistic self psychology is the anti-psychology of a Jewish or Christian psychology. Modern psychology also broke the link with the human body. In a limited way Freud recognized the body, but since then, the body has been neglected, or rejected as unimportant. What remained was the disembodied autonomous self. One sign of psychology's rejection of the body is its failure to "incorporate" male and female psychology. Again, Freud had some understanding of male and female, however limited and distorted, but none of the subsequent theorists even addressed the issue. Thus, a more accurate title for Rogers's book would be *On Becoming a Disembodied Isolated Autonomous Self.*

A Judeo-Christian theory is realistic because it is based on that which exists outside the self. To become a person is to be respectful of external realities, especially of the other person. But by making the self or autonomous individual the center of personality, all modern theories of personality remove people from reality, from the external world created by God and filled with real others. (No wonder Sartre said: "Hell is other people.") In short, these theories of the individual are intrinsically subjectivistic. A good example of this tendency is Carl Rogers, whose theory is based in a thoroughgoing subjectivism: "there are as many realities as there are persons"; we must prepare for a world of "no solid basis, a world of process and change . . . in which the mind . . . creates the new reality."[21] Other evidence of the subjectivism of much personality theory has been its reliable tendency to merge with Eastern religion, with subjective drug states, and

21. Carl Rogers, *A Way of Being* (Boston: Houghton Mifflin, 1980), p. 352.

with many kinds of occult worldviews which claim that reality is the creation of each self.

Actually, the essential logic of becoming an individual—that is, of separating and distancing the self from others—eventually gets carried to its logical extreme. First, you break the "chains" that linked you to parents, then to others, and even to society and culture. Finally, you reject the self itself; that is, you separate consciousness from the illusion of the self. You end up by rejecting the self and all its desires—and thus the process of separation culminates in an experience or state of nothingness, of total alienation. Radical autonomy ultimately means separation from everything; it means that eventually even the self is gone.

A neo-Thomist response

Implicit in the Ratzinger-Torrance treatment of substance and relation has been a criticism of Thomist philosophy as being too focused on substance. However, it is of real interest that Norris Clarke, a well-known Thomist, has recently addressed this issue.[22] He argues that the Thomist concept of substance contains within it the concept of relation. In his creative interpretation of the thought of Aquinas, he presents a strong case that the person can be understood as substance in relation, and not just as substance. If Clarke's neo-Thomist interpretation is right, this means that traditional Catholic theological philosophy represents a foundational rationale for this recent deeper and more realistic understanding of person.

In defense of the modern individual

Some positive things need to be said for the secular emphasis on independence and individuation. Freedom or independence from the

---

22. W. N. Clarke, *Person and Being* (Milwaukee: Marquette University Press, 1998).

unexamined views of others is an important virtue, not just for the secular culture but in the Judeo-Christian world as well. One of the major concerns of theology is that of free will or free choice. God gives us the freedom to choose Him—or not. From Abraham to Moses to Jesus, this theme is central to Scripture. In a certain sense, the emphasis on freedom found in the secular world of the last few centuries can be understood as the immanentizing of a basic Jewish and Christian principle: that is, the theological concept of freedom was translated into the social and political world. In any case, the importance of freedom has been a major positive contribution of modernism. Freedom by itself, for its own sake, is of course a problem. It is a major cause of alienation, isolation, and modern loneliness. But freedom for the purpose of choosing committed loving relationships is a solid moral good. Freedom is like money: it is not meant to be hoarded; it is meant to be spent—spent on love. That is, ultimately love trumps freedom.

The actual process of becoming a person: "personagenesis": the transmodern core

What is the process of becoming a person—or as Connor calls it, "personagenesis"?[23] First, this theory does not reject the person as substance but gives equal emphasis to the person as relation. In the language of Karol Wojtyła (Pope John Paul II), a person is constructed on the "metaphysical site" of substance or body, and the process of construction involves the dynamics of relationships.[24] But we should keep in mind that even relationships are partly created through the underlying neurophysiology, or body. Some scientists are now claiming that humans are hard-wired to connect with others.[25]

23. R. Connor, "The Person as Resonating Existential," *American Catholic Philosophical Quarterly* 66 (1992): p. 47.

24. Karol Wojtyła, *The Acting Person,* tran. Andrzej Potocki (Dordrecht, Holland: D. Reidel Publishing Company, 1979; original Polish edition, 1969).

25. See, for example, the emphasis accorded to oxytocin in biology today. See W. Freeman, *Societies of Brains* (Hillsdale, N.J.: Erlbaum, 1995).

The first step in personagenesis "seems to be passivity, receptivity of love from another."[26] In the natural world, this is normally the love a newborn receives from its mother. In the spiritual realm, which is at the core of person, it is listening to the call and love of God. Once initiated, the process of becoming a person continues. Wojtyła described the heart of this process as a "vertical transcendence" in which the person gives "the self to another."[27] The process of lovingly giving the self to another both transcends the self and determines the self in the act of performing loving service. The giving of the self to another is how the self is transcended; it is also how one comes to know both the other and, from the perspective of the other, to know oneself much more "objectively" than one ever can from inside an autonomous self. This process is how one becomes a person. Wojtyła noted that free will is at the center of a person's self gift to another, for while man freely determines his action, he is "at the same time fully aware" that his actions "in turn determine him; moreover they continue to determine him even when they have passed."[28]

When the other person receives one's gift of love and gives his or her self in return, the highest form of intimacy results. In this context, intimacy has been lucidly described by the philosopher Kenneth Schmitz:

> Metaphysically speaking, intimacy is not grounded in the recognition of this or that characteristic a person has, but rather in the simple unqualified presence the person is . . . Indeed, it seems to me that the presence in which intimacy is rooted is nothing short of the unique act of existing of each person. Presence is but another name for the being of something insofar as it is actual, and in intimacy we come upon and are received into the very act of existing of another. We are, then, at the heart, not only of another person, but at the very heart of the texture of being itself. No doubt it is true that the person is incommunicable in objective terms insofar as he or she is existentially

26. Connor, "The Person," p. 45.
27. Wojtyła, cited in Connor, "The Person," p. 47.
28. Wojtyła, cited in Connor, "The Person," p. 48.

unique. But in intimacy, as we approach the very act of self-disclosure, we approach the center of all communicability. It is this "secret" that we share with the other person. It is the sense of being with another at the foundation not only of our personal existence, but of being with each other in the most fundamental texture of being itself. Put in the most general terms—though we must not forget that each intimacy is through and through singular—the "secret" that we discover through intimacy is this: *that reality is not indifferent to the presence of persons.*[29]

Although Schmitz was describing the metaphysical nature of intimacy, the same understanding is at the core of psychological intimacy. Intimacy—with God and with others—thus becomes a major characteristic of a person. This intimacy is not cognitive knowledge based on abstraction, but knowledge based on experience, on union with the other.

The emphasis on mature love—that is, love which is both freely chosen and involves a serious commitment to the other, a commitment shown in self-giving—means that *friendship* is a central reality for the transmodern or religious person. Modern psychology has shown little interest in friendship; it remains to be explored in the context of this new "transmodern" psychology.

In addition, this religious understanding of the self or person brings in a concern with the development of the moral life and of the character or virtues which can maintain an integrated moral life. All of these emphases are quite different from and often contrast with the secular self's concern with autonomy, moral relativism, etc.

Addressing the postmodern critique

The postmodern criticism of the modern secular self has made some especially important points. By identifying the cultural and historical relativity of the modern self, and by underlining the moral rel-

29. Kenneth C. Schmitz, "The Geography of the Human Person," *Communio* 13 (1986): pp. 45–55, see p. 45 (emphasis in original).

ativity of the self's choices, they have clearly identified the absence of any acceptable secular rationale for self-actualization. The modern secular self, as we have seen, ignores the reality of the body and its enmeshment in the physical environment; furthermore, it omits the other and relationships as constituting the self. But, also, the modern self ignores the society in which it functions. Postmodernists push this criticism to the point of rejecting the possibility of a coherent self across different societies, cultures, and time periods. Here again, the transmodern Judeo-Christian has an answer. A transmodern or Judeo-Christian person has an absolute reference point—a kind of psychological and moral coordinate system created by the already noted two great commandments: love God and love others. These two invariants—the one "vertical," the other "horizontal"—provide a universal framework not only for the moral life but for the development of the self or person. It is a reference system which is independent of historical time or cultural location. Hence it provides a clear answer to the postmodern nihilistic and anarchic dilemma.

Christians and Jews and other theists who accept these commandments will of course work out their responses to loving God and others in personal and culturally specific ways. But these many differences in the concrete expression of different persons at different times and places should not obscure the basic system from which each person is working. Finally, through its emphasis on embodiment and on self-giving relationships, this religiously based model of the person or self also provides a satisfactory response to the modern isolated, alienated self. It is in committed loving relationships that the highest form of self—or person—comes into existence. In summary, we can now provide a definition: a transmodern person—that is, the person—is an embodied individual substance of a rational nature who is in loving relationships with others and in relationship to the outside physical world. In the mature person, the loving relationships with others are freely chosen. It remains for such an understanding to become a cultural goal.

six

Michael Novak

THE FIRST INSTITUTION OF DEMOCRACY

Tocqueville on Religion: What Faith Adds to Reason

BETTER than any other great social thinker of modern times, Tocqueville perceived in a profound and sophisticated way the crucial importance of *religion* to the modern democratic republic; and he meant by "religion" the Jewish and Christian religion. He also wrote with unparalleled clarity of the special role of the Catholic Church as a major defender of democracy. Since most secular scholars understandably lay no stress upon this central theme in Tocqueville's thought, some of what we must reflect upon today may seem new; but really it isn't. Allow me first to recall briefly some of Tocqueville's most important discoveries, and then to turn to his arresting and original views of the crucial importance of religion to democracy.

Alexis de Tocqueville was born in the wake of the sanguinary

French Revolution of 1789, into a family of the minor nobility that had suffered their share of martyrs to what the bloodthirsty were pleased to call "Reason." The circumstances of his birth assured him of certain sinecures and preferments, which by chance came to include an assignment to voyage abroad to study the prison system of the new American Republic, then not yet forty-five years old. Tocqueville completed this long voyage, including many months touring through various states of America, during the years 1831–32. Returning to France, he discovered that his report on the prisons was the least interesting part of what he had observed. He wrote that Providence had raised up in America a new model of self-governance—of liberty and equality—that was bound to sweep Europe and, indeed, the rest of the world.[1] He felt an obligation to try to understand what was coming, and to prepare his fellow Europeans for it, the French of course most of all. What constituted this new model? What were its principles and its preconditions? What were its weaknesses, and its likely fate?

Around the world, Tocqueville is regarded as a genius who wrote more intelligently about the American experiment than anyone before or since. No fewer than four English translations of *Democracy in America* have appeared in America over the years, the latest having arrived from the hands of the eminent political philosopher from Harvard Harvey Mansfield and his wife and fellow scholar, Delba Winthrop.[2]

No one has ever traced in more elegant detail the subtle differences

1. Tocqueville wrote in his Author's Introduction: "If patient observation and sincere meditation have led men of the present day to recognize that both the past and the future of their history consist in the gradual and measured advance of equality, that discovery in itself gives this progress the sacred character of the will of the Sovereign Master. In that case effort to halt democracy appears as a fight against God Himself, and nations have no alternative but to acquiesce in the social state imposed by Providence." *Democracy in America,* trans. George Lawrence, ed. J. P. Mayer (New York: Anchor Books, 1969), p. 12.

2. The English translations of *Democracy in America* are: the Henry Reeve (1838) text revised by Francis Bowen (1862), now further corrected and edited with a

of imagination, sensibility, habits, and expectations engendered by life in an aristocratic order, as compared with those engulfed by a democratic order; no one paid more attention to the strong and weak points of each than Tocqueville.[3] No one saw more clearly the concrete, lived meaning of *"equality"* in the new order;[4] and the precise lineaments of that new phenomenon in human history, the democratic *"individual,"* which had no exact counterpart in European cultures.[5]

---

historical essay, editorial notes, and bibliographies by Philip Bradley (New York: Vintage Books, 1945); the George Lawrence translation, ed. J. P. Mayer (New York: Anchor Books, 1969); and the translation by Harvey C. Mansfield and Delba Winthrop (Chicago: University of Chicago Press, 2000).

3. Among many other passages: "Among democratic peoples new families continually rise from nothing while others fall, and nobody's position is quite stable. The woof of time is ever being broken and the track of past generations lost. Those who have gone before are easily forgotten, and no one gives a thought to those who will follow. All a man's interests are limited to those near himself.

"As each class catches up with the next and gets mixed with it, its members do not care about one another as strangers. Aristocracy links everybody, from peasant to king, in one long chain. Democracy breaks the chain and frees each link.

"As social equality spreads there are more and more people who, though neither rich nor powerful enough to have much hold over others, have gained or kept enough wealth and enough understanding to look after their own needs. Such folk owe no man anything and hardly expect anything from anybody. They form the habit of thinking of themselves in isolation and imagine that their whole destiny is in their own hands." Lawrence and Mayer, *Democracy in America*, pp. 507–8.

4. Tocqueville's focus on "equality" begins early in his volume and pervades the whole: "The gradual development of the principle of equality is a providential fact. It has all the chief characteristics of such a fact: it is universal, it is durable, it constantly eludes all human interference, and all events as well as all men contribute to its progress." Mansfield and Winthrop, *Democracy in America*, p. 6. This translation is better than the Lawrence text: "Therefore the gradual progress of equality is something fated. The main features of this progress are the following: it is universal and permanent, it is daily passing beyond human control and every event and every man helps it along." Lawrence and Mayer, *Democracy in America*, p. 12.

5. "'Individualism' is a word recently coined to express a new idea. Our fathers only knew about egoism. Egoism is a passionate and exaggerated love of self which leads a man to think of all things in terms of himself and to prefer himself to all.

"Individualism is a calm and considered feeling which disposes each citizen to isolate himself from the mass of his fellows and withdraw into the circle of family and

Tocqueville also grasped the extraordinary pervasiveness of *voluntary associations* in the daily texture of American life, as a social force far more potent and extensive than the state. What the French turn to *"l'état"* to do, he wrote, and the English turn to the aristocracy to do, the Americans do by turning to one another and forming an association.[6] It is through associations that Americans practice self-government, he said; they do not depend on government, they organize themselves to accomplish their own ends. He concluded that the law of association is the first law of democracy.[7] He did not think that there were ten men in all of France in 1835 who had the habit of forming associations as the Americans did every day.[8]

Tocqueville feared that, in the end, the experiment in democracy would finish in tyranny, when the lust of democrats for equality led them to demand such an extensive governmental network of services to remove the insecurities, edges, and hardships from life that they would be ensnared under a new "soft despotism."[9]

---

friends; with this little society formed to his taste, he gladly leaves the greater society to look after itself." Lawrence and Mayer, *Democracy in America*, p. 506.

6. Ibid., p. 517.

7. "Nothing, in my view, more deserves attention than the intellectual and moral associations in America. American political and industrial associations easily catch our eyes, but the others tend not to be noticed. And even if we do notice them we tend to misunderstand them, hardly ever having seen anything similar before. However, we should recognize that the latter are as necessary as the former to the American people; perhaps more so.

"In democratic countries knowledge of how to combine is the mother of all other forms of knowledge; on its progress depends that of all the others.

"Among laws controlling human societies there is one more precise and clearer, it seems to me, than all the others. If men are to remain civilized or to become civilized, the art of association must develop and improve among them at the same speed as equality of conditions spreads." Ibid., p. 517.

8. "When the Revolution started, it would have been impossible to find, in most parts of France, even ten men who before the Revolution were used to acting in concert and defending their interests without appealing to the central power for aid." Alexis de Tocqueville, *The Old Regime and the French Revolution,* trans. Stuart Gilbert (Garden City, N.Y.: Doubleday, 1955), p. 206.

9. "I am trying to imagine under what novel features *despotism* may appear in the

Americans of all persuasions have found Tocqueville's prediction of the inevitable contradiction between liberty and equality sobering. Even the partisans of ever greater equality are careful to couch their appeals in terms of "choice," thinking in that way to avoid the inevitable collision. Those of us who are known as neoconservatives[10] (or,

---

world. In the first place, I see an innumerable multitude of men, alike and equal, constantly circling around in pursuit of the petty and banal pleasures with which they glut their souls. Each one of them, withdrawn into himself, is almost unaware of the fate of the rest . . .

"Over this kind of men stands an immense, protective power which is alone responsible for securing their enjoyment and watching over their fate. That power is absolute, thoughtful of detail, orderly, provident, and gentle. It would resemble parental authority if, fatherlike, it tried to prepare its charges for a man's life, but on the contrary, it only tries to keep them in perpetual childhood. It likes to see the citizens enjoy themselves, provided that they think of nothing but enjoyment. It gladly works for their happiness but wants to be sole agent and judge of it. It provides for their security, foresees and supplies their necessities, facilitates their pleasure, manages their principal concerns, directs their industry, makes rules for their testaments, and divides their inheritances. Why should it not entirely relieve them from the trouble of thinking and all the cares of living?

"Thus it daily makes the exercise of free choice less useful and rarer, restricts the activity of free will within a narrower compass, and little by little robs each citizen of the proper use of his own faculties. Equality has prepared men for all this, predisposing them to endure it and often even regard it as beneficial.

"Having thus taken each citizen in turn in its powerful grasp and shaped him to its will, government then extends its embrace to include the whole of society. It covers the whole of social life with a network of petty, complicated rules that are both minute and uniform, through which even men of the greatest originality and the most vigorous temperament cannot force their heads above the crowd. It does not break men's will, but softens, bends, and guides it; it seldom enjoins, but often inhibits, action; it does not destroy anything, but prevents much being born; it is not at all tyrannical, but it hinders, restrains, enervates, stifles, and stultifies *so much that in the end each nation is no more than a flock of timid and hardworking animals with the government as its shepherd.*" Lawrence and Mayer, *Democracy in America,* pp. 691–92 [emphasis added].

10. The necessity of the free market, the limited priority of politics over economics, and the primacy of the spirit—that is a fairly good summary of the neoconservative position, as outlined in Irving Kristol's *Reflections of a Neoconservative: Looking Back, Looking Ahead* (New York: Basic Books, 1983). See also his *Neoconservatism: Selected Essays 1949–1995* (New York: Free Press, 1995).

as I prefer, whigs),[11] believe that Tocqueville presciently foresaw precisely that state of willing servility into which the welfare state of social democracy has been inexorably leading us.

Tocqueville was also uncommonly astute in his analysis of the totally different meanings of "self-interest" in Europe, rooted in an aristocratic moral vision, and in America.[12] The European aristocratic vision of life is at root Catholic, feudal, Thomistic, Aristotelian, Greek. A sharp distinction is drawn between those things that are mere means, vulgar and servile, and those that are ends-in-themselves and noble. The liberal arts, for instance, are distinguished from the servile, manual, mechanical arts. A related distinction is drawn between deeds that are merely useful and those that are beautiful. The truly good is contrasted with the merely utilitarian; so also the noble with the servile. As much as possible, people of noble rank devote themselves to the cultivation of the beautiful, the good, ends in themselves.

11. For more on the Catholic Whig tradition see Michael Novak, "Thomas Aquinas, the First Whig," in *This Hemisphere of Liberty* (Washington, D.C.: AEI Press, 1992), pp. 107–12. See also "The Catholic Whig Revisited," *First Things* (March 1990), reprinted in *On Cultivating Liberty* (Lanham, Md.: Rowman & Littlefield, 1999).

12. "When the world was under the control of a few rich and powerful men, they liked to entertain a sublime conception of the duties of man. It gratified them to make out that it is a glorious thing to forget oneself and that one should do good without self-interest, as God himself does. That was the official doctrine of morality at that time.

"I doubt whether men were better in times of aristocracy than at other times, but certainly they talked continually about the beauties of virtue. Only in secret did they study its utility. But since imagination has been taking less lofty flights, and every man's thoughts are centered on himself, moralists take fright at this idea of sacrifice and no longer venture to suggest it for consideration. So they are reduced to inquiring whether it is not to the individual advantage of each to work for the good of all, and when they have found one of those points where private advantage does meet and coincide with the general interest, they eagerly call attention thereto. Thus what was an isolated observation becomes a general doctrine, and in the end one comes to believe that one sees that by serving his fellows man serves himself and that doing good is to his private advantage." Lawrence and Mayer, *Democracy in America*, p. 525. See also Michael Novak, ch. 2 on Madison and Tocqueville on "self-interest," in *Free Persons and the Common Good* (Lanham, Md.: Madison Books, 1989).

The ways and means to their ends are supplied by their inferiors, to whom belongs the servile work. *Noblesse oblige.*

All these traditional distinctions have their proper validity and all make an important point, which Tocqueville does not mean to deny. Nonetheless, his own eyes and ears have revealed to him that Americans have an altogether different way of speaking about self-interest.[13] Practically every American, being a descendant of immigrants, knows that the same quantum of work performed in America as elsewhere reaps him a more ample reward. Clearly, it was not personal effort alone that led to the increase. The system is more beneficent than those their families had experienced elsewhere, and for this discernible difference in blessings he or she gives thanks for the system. Thus virtually every American, by the same measure, is sensible of an obligation to contribute to the common good, in order to assure the continuance of this same beneficent system into the future. Americans imagine that it is in their own interest to make contributions to the common welfare and the public good, Tocqueville observes; it is more than a duty, since it inures to their own future benefit and that of their children.

Americans consider the public good to be their own personal good, and they link their own self-interest to the public good.

Every day, Tocqueville notes, Americans perform generous deeds for the common good, but they do not describe these as deeds performed for the common good; they describe them as deeds performed in their own self-interest, broadly understood. They do not

---

13. "The Americans, on the other hand, enjoy explaining almost every act of their lives on the principle of self-interest properly understood. It gives them pleasure to point out how an enlightened self-love continually leads them to help one another and disposes them freely to give part of their time and wealth for the good of the state. I think that in this they often do themselves less than justice, for sometimes in the United States, as elsewhere, one sees people carried away by the disinterested, spontaneous impulses natural to man. But the Americans are hardly prepared to admit that they do give way to emotions of this sort. They prefer to give the credit to their philosophy rather than to themselves." Lawrence and Mayer, *Democracy in America*, p. 526.

speak, Tocqueville says, of beauty but of utility.[14] They never speak of solidarity, but of self-interest. Clearly, this is a novel type of self-interest, Tocqueville deduces, and he calls it by a novel name, *self-interest rightly understood*. Europeans formed to aristocratic manners, he notes, disdain the merely useful and the motive of self-interest.

Americans, on the contrary, are pleased to explain almost all the actions of their life with the aid of self-interest well understood; they complacently show how the enlightened love of themselves constantly brings them to aid each other and disposes them willingly to sacrifice a part of their time and their wealth to the good of the state.[15]

In fact, he notes, Americans are likely to insist that they are acting from self-interest even when by European standards they are not.

In short, Tocqueville discerned with great delicacy and uncanny perspicacity the many subtle and powerful ways by which the inner life of Americans differed from that of Europeans in his time—and still does today, I believe, despite the many convergences of the intervening generations.

Nonetheless, Tocqueville wrote as a Catholic. Indeed, it is highly unlikely that any mind unformed by the Catholic tradition would have so readily discerned, and been able to articulate, the subtle differences between the new democratic way of life and the Catholic aristocratic roots of European thought and sensibilities. Precisely because America was Protestant in sensibility and Tocqueville Catholic, his sensitivity and fine intelligence took note of minute differences in the slightest vibrations of the soul. He came to America as an outsider not only because he was French and aristocratic, but also because he was Catholic. In his book, in fact, he described himself as a practicing Catholic who, on this account, came into frequent contact with Cath-

14. "In the United States there is hardly any talk of the beauty of virtue. But they maintain that virtue is useful and prove it every day. American moralists do not pretend that one must sacrifice himself for his fellows because it is a fine thing to do so. But they boldly assert that such sacrifice is as necessary for the man who makes it as for the beneficiaries." Ibid., p. 525.

15. Ibid., p. 502.

olic priests wherever he went in America, and had many long and intelligent conversations with them.[16] He learned to see America from their vantage point, too, and thus drew on a perspective that he and they partly shared in common (since the Catholic theology studied by the priests of the time—often in Europe—is necessarily steeped in the intellectual origins of European culture).

Along with Tocqueville, in fact, virtually all other Catholic visitors to America also discovered in the United States a fresh way of thinking about Catholicism, which seemed to reveal new possibilities in their faith, as if in America it might achieve a more fundamental self-expression than it had ever achieved in Europe. For at least two ideas at the heart of the American experiment are also at the heart of the Catholic faith: the twin ideas of the common *equality* of all men and women (whatever their rank) before the face of God, and the high *dignity* of the individual, who has been given by the Creator the awesome liberty to say *yes* or *no,* to choose his or her own destiny. In the Catholic faith humans are the only creatures in this world who are, as images of God, ends in themselves, not means.[17]

In this recognition of America as a homeland of their souls, Toc-

16. "I questioned the faithful of all communions; I particularly sought the society of clergymen, who are the depositaries of the various creeds and have a personal interest in their survival. *As a practicing Catholic I was particularly close to the Catholic priests, with some of whom I soon established a certain intimacy.* I expressed my astonishment and revealed my doubts to each of them; I found that they all agreed with each other except about details; all thought that the main reason for the quiet sway of religion over their country was the complete separation of church and state. I have no hesitation in stating that throughout my stay in America I met nobody, lay or cleric, who did not agree about that." Ibid., p. 295 [emphasis added].

17. "Person signifies what is noblest in the whole of nature" (*Summa theologiae* Ia q. 29, a. 2). "Among substances the individual merits a special name, and so is termed hypostasis, suppositum, or first substance. Particular individuals have a still more special and perfect existence in rational substances who are masters of their own activity and act of themselves, unlike other things which are acted upon. Therefore singular rational substances receive the special name of persons" (*Summa theologiae* Ia q. 19, a. 1). "An individual who is governed for the sake of the species is not governed because of any inherent worth. But human persons come under divine providence in their own

queville was like Philip Mazzei, the Marquis de Lafayette, Kosciuszko, Pulaski, and others who befriended the revolutionary generation of Americans and cast their lot with them; and like many European visitors before and since, who have written on the meaning of America, such as Michel de Crevecoeur, Jacques Maritain and Raymond Bruckberger, Raimundo Pezzamenti, Rocco Buttiglione, Michael Zoeller, and others.[18] We are confronted, therefore, with the great importance for democracy that Tocqueville ascribed to religion.

1. Religion is the first political institution of democracy

Tocqueville claimed that the first of the political institutions of the Americans was their religion. This claim has always seemed odd to those secular writers who accept the secularization thesis, namely, that the main trend of the modern era is the decline of religion vis-à-vis an ascendant secular philosophy. In the main, secular writers have explained Tocqueville's claim by interpreting it as a comment on an earlier historical stage in which, admittedly, religion was highly visible and vocal. Unfortunately for this thesis, however, empirically, religion has not grown more impotent in recent times. On the contrary, in region after region, religion seems more dynamic, and the secular tendency weaker and less self-assured, than at any time in the last two hundred years.[19] In the United States, it appears that more Amer-

right, for the activities of rational creatures alone are divinely directed for the sake of the individual as well as of the species" (*III Summa contra gentiles*, 113). St. *Thomas Aquinas, Philosophical Texts*, trans. Thomas Gilby (New York: Oxford University Press, 1960), pp. 389, 392.

The historical emergence of personal dignity was beautifully treated by Jacques Maritain with respect to the arts in *Creative Intuition in Art and Poetry*, Bollinger Series (New York: Pantheon Books, 1953); and with respect to politics in *The Person and the Common Good*, trans. John J. Fitzgerald (New York: Charles Scribner's Sons, 1947).

18. Two important books on this theme are: Jacques Maritain, *Reflections on America* (New York: Scribner, 1958), and Raymond-Léopold Bruckberger, *Image of America*, trans. C. G. Paulding and Virgilia Peterson (New York: Viking Press, 1959).

19. The first major summary of the evidence against the secularization thesis is

icans go to church and engage in daily or weekly religious activities than in 1776.[20] Over any given weekend in the autumn, more Americans attend church, synagogue, or mosque than attend all the football games (professional, college, and secondary school) in the nation; more attend church in person, even, than watch football on *television* Saturday and Sunday. The religious factor is highly potent in American electoral politics, some would even say the single most important factor today.[21] The pro-life movement, for instance, is the largest

---

found in Richard John Neuhaus, *Unsecular America* (Grand Rapids, Mich.: William B. Eerdmans Publishing Company, 1986).

20. See Michael Medved's apt summary: "As *Newsweek* magazine reported in January 1992: 'This week, if you believe at all in opinion surveys, more of us will pray than will go to work, or exercise, or have sexual relations.' According to *Newsweek*'s research, 78 percent of Americans pray at least once a week, and more than 40 percent attend worship services on a weekly basis. *This means that the number of people who go to church in a given week is more than five times larger than the number of people who go to the movies.*

"Perhaps most astonishing of all, a poll reported in *U.S. News and World Report* (December 1991) asked American voters to describe 'their greatest objective in life'; fully 56 percent listed 'a closer relationship to God' as their top personal priority." *Hollywood vs. America: Popular Culture and the War on Traditional Values* (New York: Harper Collins, 1992), p. 71. Medved also cites Gallup and other polling data.

A November 29–30, 2005, Fox News/Opinion Dynamics poll of 900 registered voters nationwide revealed that 42 percent attend church, synagogue, or another place of worship at least once a week, and another 12 percent attend almost every week. Sixty-seven percent report that they pray every day. (Available online at www.foxnews.com/projects/pdf/poll_religion.pdf)

21. The survey done by John Green for the Pew Charitable Trust shows that religious traditions do matter in politics. He summarizes the result as follows: "84 percent of observant white evangelical Protestants voted for Bush . . . Less observant white evangelical Protestants did not vote as strongly Republican, just 55 percent . . . With Roman Catholics, a pattern continues that had been developing all through the 1990s: more observant Roman Catholics voted more Republican, less observant more Democratic . . . In contrast to their white counterparts, black Protestants voted overwhelmingly for Gore: 96 percent. Of course, African Americans generally vote Democratic, but the black Protestant church is the strongest Democratic component of the African American community. Hispanics voted for Gore as well, particularly Hispanic Catholics, at 76 percent. Hispanic Protestants were a little more divided but still gave Gore 67 percent of their votes." "How the Faithful Voted," *Center Conversations,* published by

and best-organized such movement in the world (this movement of course includes some atheists).

A second shocking claim of Tocqueville—admittedly more an implicit suggestion than an outright proposition—is that one day Catholics might be in the best intellectual position to explain and defend the presuppositions of democracy. Recently, Pierre Manent of France, a Tocqueville scholar himself, noted that the church has been better able over the last century to adapt itself to democracy than secular democracy to religion; and the church, regarding the future, may be in a more assertive, creative, optimistic mode than the secular democracies.[22] I would add that the premises of Catholic faith include the premises of democracy, while the premises of secular thought, left to itself, not only do not suffice for the defense of the premises of democ-

the Ethics and Public Policy Center, March 2001, no. 10, p. 2. On the Catholic vote, see Steve Wagner, "Election 2000," *Crisis* (January 2001): pp. 10–16.

Results from the 2004 presidential election revealed the following: "Overall, Evangelical Protestants strongly backed Bush with 78 percent of their votes . . . Traditionalist Evangelicals (highly orthodox beliefs and practices) voted 88 percent for Bush . . . Mainline Protestants divided their votes evenly, with Bush and Kerry each receiving 50 percent . . . Modernist Mainline Protestants strongly backed Kerry with 78 percent . . . Black Protestants strongly backed Kerry with 83 percent . . . Traditionalist Catholics strongly preferred Bush with 72 percent . . . In contrast, Modernist Catholics were strongly for Kerry, with 69 percent." John C. Green, Corwin E. Smidt, James L. Guth, and Lyman A. Kellstedt, "The American Religious Landscape and the 2004 Presidential Vote: Increased Polarization." Pew Forum on Religion and Public Life, January 2005.

22. Manent's final paragraph: "[T]he political submission of the Church to democracy is, perhaps, finally, a fortunate one. The Church willy-nilly conformed herself to all of democracy's demands. Democracy no longer, in good faith, has any essential reproach to make against the Church. From now on it can hear the question the Church poses, the question which it alone poses, the question *Quid sit homo*—What is man? But democracy neither wants to nor can respond to this question in any manner or form. On democracy's side of the scale, we are left with political sovereignty and dialectical impotence. On the Church's side, we are left with political submission and dialectical advantage. The relation unleashed by the Enlightenment is today reversed. No one knows what will happen when democracy and the Church become aware of this reversal." Pierre Manent, "Christianity and Democracy," in *A Free Society Reader*, ed. Michael Novak, William Brailsford, and Cornelis Heesters (Lanham, Md.: Lexington Books, 2000), p. 125.

racy, but actually undermine them. On what generally agreed grounds today, for example, do secular philosophers defend human rights or the distinctive dignity of human beings among other creatures?

However that may be, even if we were to concede that secular philosophy is perfectly adequate to the defense of democracy, still, many today are no longer persuaded that a merely secular philosophy offers a credible philosophy of human destiny. Among such people, the suggestion of Tocqueville that over time the Catholic faith would prove to be an important ally of democracy has been too little discussed. "America," he wrote,

> is the most democratic country in the world, and at the same time, according to reliable reports, it is the country in which the Roman Catholic religion is making the most progress ... If Catholicism could ultimately escape from the political animosities to which it has given rise [in Europe, carried over into America], I am almost certain that that same spirit of the age which now seems so contrary to it would turn into a powerful ally, and that it would suddenly make great conquests.[23]

What is it about the Jewish and Christian religions, in particular Catholicism, that led Tocqueville to see them as the primary political institution of democracy? The first reason is their powerful conviction about *the centrality of human liberty* to the entire purpose of the universe. The axis of creation is human liberty and destiny; every story in the Bible confirms this. The primacy of liberty is the very ground not only of the whig view of the world. The Bible, too, understands liberty in a way that lends human persons unsurpassed dignity. In addition, it understands liberty as the opposite of license, as the triumph of practical reason over animal instinct, as self-government and self-mastery over libertinism. It is not an accident that descendants of Tocqueville and Rochambeau were among those Frenchmen who designed the Statue of Liberty as a tribute to the American idea

23. Lawrence and Mayer, *Democracy in America*, p. 450.

of liberty: a sober woman with the torch of *reason* raised aloft with one arm, and the book of the *law* clasped in the other—*reason* over passion, bigotry, and ignorance; and liberty under *law*.[24]

But the dignity of the free person is not the only underpinning that Catholicism gives to democracy. It also offers a thorough and profound underpinning to the idea of *equality*. For equality is not (in an empirical sense) an idea reached by natural reason. When the Athenians bade the citizens of Melos to treat with them in a spirit of equality, they received the following scornful reply:

> You know as well as we do that right, as the world goes, is only in question between equals in power, while the strong do what they can and the weak suffer what they must.[25]

Yet the Hebrew tradition introduced to the whole world by Christians taught a different lesson: that in the eyes of our Creator, all men and women of whatever station or rank are equal. This Judge is impressed neither by power nor wealth nor position. In nature, some are strong and some are weak, some handsome and some plain, some richly talented and others not. He calls every one, equally, to be His friend. If humans are equal, therefore, it is solely in His eyes. The Catholic faith, Tocqueville observes, over many centuries firmly established the idea of equality in the consciousness of the world:

> Among the various Christian doctrines Catholicism seems one of those most favorable to equality of conditions. For Catholics religious society is composed of two elements: priest and people. The priest is raised above the faithful; all below him are equal.
>
> In matters of dogma the Catholic faith places all intellects on the same level; the learned man and the ignorant, the genius and the common herd, must all subscribe to the same details of beliefs; rich and poor must follow the same observances, and it imposes the same

24. Barry Moreno, *The Statue of Liberty Encyclopedia* (New York: Simon & Schuster, 2000).

25. Thucydides, *The Peloponnesian Wars* (New York: Modern Library, 1951), p. 331.

austerities upon the strong and the weak; it makes no compromise with any mortal, but applying the same standard to every human being, it mingles all classes of society at the foot of the same altar, just as they are mingled in the sight of God.

Catholicism may dispose the faithful to obedience, but it does not prepare them for inequality. However, I would say that Protestantism in general orients men much less toward equality than toward independence.[26]

In addition, the Catholic faith emphasizes the incommensurable value of the human person through its teaching on the immortality of the soul. This teaching bathes human rights in a brilliant light. Human rights arise not just from nature but from the higher destiny with which God gifted humans. As Alexander Hamilton wrote:

> Moral obligation, according to [Hobbes], is derived from the introduction of civil society; and there is no virtue but what is purely artificial, the mere contrivance of politicians, for the maintenance of social intercourse. But the reason he ran into this absurd and impious doctrine was that he disbelieved the existence of an intelligent superintending principle, who is the governor and will be the final judge of the universe . . .
>
> To grant that there is a supreme intelligence who rules the world and has established laws to regulate the actions of his creatures; and still to assert that man, in a state of nature, may be considered as perfectly free from all restraints of law and government, appears to a common understanding altogether irreconcilable. Good and wise men, in all ages, have embraced a very dissimilar theory. They have supposed that *the deity, from the relations we stand in to himself and to each other, has constituted an eternal and immutable law, which is indispensably obligatory upon all mankind, prior to any human institution whatever.* This is what is called the law of nature . . . Upon this law depend the natural rights of mankind.[27] [emphasis added]

26. Lawrence and Mayer, *Democracy in America,* p. 288.

27. "The Farmer Refuted" (1775), in *Papers,* ed. Harold C. Syrett (New York: Columbia University Press, 1961), vol. 1, p. 87, as quoted by Thomas West, Salvatori lecture.

Take away the immortality of the soul, and it is difficult to establish the dignity of man any higher than that of any other animal. Even if such a difficult philosophical task is successful, its result is not likely to have the radiance that it would gain from Jewish and Christian faith.

It is obvious, then, that if the foundations of democracy lie in the three principles of (1) the dignity of the free person, (2) the equality of all in the eyes of God, and (3) the immortal value of every person before God, democracy owes an enormous debt to Jewish and Christian faith. This point may not be obvious to those to whom President Washington referred in his "Farewell Address" as "minds of peculiar structure,"[28] but for large majorities, including many of the most brilliant and learned, faith adds powerful arguments to the weaker arguments presented by philosophy, on the three great questions: of human dignity, equality, and immortal value.

2. What does faith add to reason?

Beyond noting that religion is the first political institution of democracy because of the fundamental principles it lowers into place, Tocqueville also notes that Jewish and Christian faith adds several other indispensable benefits to democratic experiments.

First, faith corrects morals and manners. As an ill-fated bill in the Virginia Assembly put it in 1784, "The general diffusion of Christian knowledge hath a tendency to correct the morals of men, restraining their vices, and preserve the peace of society."[29] Although Americans are bold and enterprising in making their fortunes, Tocqueville writes:

---

28. George Washington, "Farewell Address," in *George Washington: A Collection,* ed. W. B. Allen (Indianapolis: Liberty Classics, 1988), p. 521.

29. From "A Bill Establishing a Provision for Teachers of the Christian Religion," quoted in John Eidsmoe, *Christianity and the Constitution: The Faith of Our Founding Fathers* (Grand Rapids, Mich.: Baker Books, 1987), p. 310.

American revolutionaries are obliged ostensibly to profess a certain respect for Christian morality and equity, and that does not allow them
easily to break the laws when those are opposed to the executions of
their designs; nor would they find it easy to surmount the scruples of
their partisans even if they were able to get over their own. Up till now
no one in the United States has dared to profess the maxim that everything is allowed in the interests of society, an impious maxim apparently invented . . . to legitimatize every future tyrant.[30]

Thus, while in a free society "the law allows the American people to do everything, there are things which religion prevents them
from imagining and forbids them to dare"[31]—such as breaking the
law. When consciences are active, policemen need be few; citizens are
law-abiding willingly. Colonial Americans had already experienced
periods of declines in religion, accompanied by a steady moral decline. They had also seen religious awakenings lead to tangible im-
provements in social peace. This is why they all believed that religion
is "necessary to the maintenance of republican institutions. That is
not the view of one class or party among the citizens, but of the whole
nation; it is found in all ranks."[32]

Second, Tocqueville noted: "*Fixed ideas about God and human
nature are indispensable* to men for the conduct of daily life, and it is
daily life that prevents them from acquiring them."[33] But these "fixed
ideas" are difficult for most men to reach. Even great philosophers
stumble in trying to come to them. But biblical faith provides to reason something that only a very few philosophers, and they only un-
certainly, can reach for themselves. Thus, sound religion, tested in
long experience, gives a culture an immense advantage. For men cannot act without living out general ideas. Clarity of soul prevents ener-
vation and the dissipation of energies. Some ideas, Tocqueville writes,
are a particular boon to free men: ideas rooted in the unity of hu-

30. Lawrence and Mayer, *Democracy in America*, p. 292. It is here that Tocqueville
calls religion "the first of their political institutions." A powerful phrase.
31. Ibid.   32. Ibid., p. 293.
33. Ibid., p. 443.

mankind, duties to neighbor, truth, honesty, and love for the law of reason. Regarding these essential ideas, the answers biblical religion gives are "clear, precise, intelligible to the crowd, and very durable."[34]

Third, religion adds to reason indispensable support for the view that every human being is not simply a bundle of pleasures and pains, a higher kind of cow or kitten or other contented domestic animal. "Democracy favors the taste for physical pleasures," Tocqueville writes. "This taste, if it becomes excessive, soon disposes men to believe that nothing but matter exists. Materialism, in its turn, spurs them on to such delights with mad impetuosity. Such is the vicious circle into which democratic nations are driven. It is good that they see the danger and draw back."[35]

The principle of equality that animates democracies, pulling men downwards, will slowly destroy what is most human in them, their souls. It is religion that checks and reverses this process and, more than that, spurs greatness, Tocqueville thinks. Faith sows its good effects in art and manners, as well as in the arena of practical action. Belief in immortality prods humans to aspire upwards, and in this way grounds their awareness of their own special dignity and natural rights.

Fourth, faith adds to a morality of mere reason an acute sense of *acting in the presence of a personal and undeceivable Judge,* Who sees and knows even actions performed in secret, even willful acts committed solely in one's heart. Thus, faith adds motives for maintaining high standards, and for seeking to do things perfectly *even when no one is looking.* Faith gives us reasons to paint the bottom of the chair, and clean the unseen corners of a room: godliness entails attention to details that no one but God sees. Whereas morality construed within the bounds of reason alone is, at best, a matter of utilitarian calculation or deontological rules, faith sees moral behavior in terms of relations between two persons, ourselves and the God to Whom we owe much. In this vein, Ben Franklin chastised his colleagues at the Con-

34. Ibid., pp. 442–46.
35. Ibid., pp. 542ff.

stitutional Convention for their ingratitude to their beneficent Friend
Who had assisted them when they were in need.

> In this situation of this Assembly, groping as it were in the dark to find
> political truth, and scarce able to distinguish it when presented to us,
> how has it happened, Sir, that we have not hitherto once thought of
> humbly applying to the Father of lights to illuminate our understand-
> ings? In the beginning of the contest with G. Britain, when we were
> sensible of danger we had daily prayer in this room for the divine
> protection.—Our prayers, Sir, were heard, and they were graciously
> answered. All of us who were engaged in the struggle must have ob-
> served frequent instances of superintending providence in our favor.
> To that kind providence we owe this happy opportunity of consulting
> in peace on the means of establishing our future national felicity. And
> have we now forgotten that powerful friend? Or do we imagine that
> we no longer need his assistance? I have lived, Sir, a long time, and
> the longer I live, the more convincing proofs I see of this truth—*that
> God governs in the affairs of men.*[36] [emphasis in the original]

Fifth, in America, Tocqueville writes, religion *"reigns supreme in
the souls of women, and it is women who shape mores."* Faith in America has had a dramatic effect on mores, especially in the home. "Certainly, of all the countries in the world, America is the one in which
the marriage tie is most respected and where the highest and truest
conception of conjugal happiness has been conceived." Tocqueville
has no doubt that the "great severity of mores which one notices in
the United States has its primary origin in beliefs." The comparative
laxity of morals in Europe breeds mistrust even in the home, and even
broader ripples of mistrust in the public sphere beyond the home.

> In Europe almost all the disorders of society are born around the do-
> mestic hearth and not far from the nuptial bed. It is there that men
> come to feel scorn for natural ties and legitimate pleasures and de-
> velop a taste for disorder, restlessness of spirit, and instability of de-

---

36. Quoted by James Madison, *Notes of Debates in the Federal Convention of 1787*
(New York: W. W. Norton and Company, 1987), pp. 209–10.

sires. Shaken by the tumultuous passions which have often troubled his own house, the European finds it hard to submit to the authority of the state's legislators.[37]

When there is no trust in the home, trust in public life is highly improbable. Where there is a lack of self-government at home, self-government in the public sphere has little probability of success. If one cannot say "that in the United States religion influences the laws or political opinions in detail," Tocqueville continues, "it does direct mores, and by regulating domestic life it helps to regulate the state."[38]

In sum, to say nothing of otherworldly benefits, Tocqueville argues that faith adds to reason five worldly strengths: (1) *restraint of vice* and gains in social peace; (2) fixed, stable, and *general ideas* about the dynamics of life; (3) *a check on the downward bias* of the principle of equality and the materialism toward which it gravitates; (4) a new conception of *morality as a personal relation* with our Creator, and thus *a motive for acting well even when no one is looking;* and (5) through *the high honor paid to the marriage bond,* the *quiet regulation of mores* in marriage and in the home.

3. *The spirit of religion and the spirit of liberty*

One of Tocqueville's most penetrating passages has always touched me very deeply, ever since I was a young man. This is his passage on the historically novel combination of *the spirit of religion and the spirit of freedom.* The passage deserves to be read in its entirety, but I here content myself with an excerpt:

> I have already said enough to put Anglo-American civilization in its true light. It is the product of two perfectly distinct elements which elsewhere have often been at war with one another but which in America it was somehow possible to incorporate into each other, forming a marvelous combination. I mean the *spirit of religion* and

37. Lawrence and Mayer, *Democracy in America,* p. 291.
38. Ibid.

the *spirit of freedom* . . . Far from harming each other, these two apparently opposed tendencies work in harmony and seem to lend mutual support.

Religion regards civil liberty as a noble exercise of men's faculties, the world of politics being a sphere intended by the Creator for the free play of intelligence. Religion, being free and powerful within its own sphere and content with the position reserved for it, realized that its sway is all the better established because it relies only on its own powers and rules men's hearts without external support.

Freedom sees religion as the companion of its struggles and triumphs, the cradle of its infancy, and the divine source of its rights. Religion is considered as the guardian of mores, and mores are regarded as the guarantee of the laws and pledge for the maintenance of freedom itself.[39]

What are the implications of these Tocquevillian insights today? First, that the Catholic faith puts in place three crucial pre-conditions of democracy: truth, freedom, and dignity. Enunciated in a little more detail, these three ideas are: a strong idea of *truth,* in the sense of a regulative ideal of our minds driving our inquiries to weed out all that is bogus, false, and unworthy of reasoned assent; a moral conception of human *freedom;* and a profound sense of the *dignity* and nobility of the human being, body and soul. These are the three background beliefs that make intelligible the conception of human rights and the spiritual primacy of liberty.

Without the regulative ideal of truth, the practice of liberty lapses into license, and self-government decays into self-indulgence.

From Tocqueville's point of view, the spirit of religion is indispensable to the successful incarnation of the spirit of liberty. That was also, he noted, the view of the early Americans without exception.

Yet these ideas, Tocqueville argued, are not American. They are universal. They are global. They are catholic (small "c").

39. Ibid., pp. 46–47.

seven

Romanus Cessario

MORAL REALISM AND CHRISTIAN VALUES

WHAT can a professor of theology from Boston add to this series of essays, which includes work by an Oxford fellow, distinguished professors of jurisprudence representing the Judaeo-
Christian tradition, a New York psychologist, an eminent Canadian
philosopher—some consider him the best Catholic philosopher in
the world—and my good friend Michael Novak, whose *chef-d'oeuvre*
ranks, we are told, among "those rare books that actually [have]
changed the world." The answer to this question illuminates something important about the nature of theology. Theology is the only
science that depends on a truth that it receives rather than one that
it discovers. Even a modest theologian, when he remains true to his
discipline and to his ecclesial vocation, can represent the claims of
faith to the philosophical disciplines. The subtitle of the present lecture series indicates that the Institute for the Psychological Sciences

adopts a broad posture: "Faith and Values within the Secular State."
As a Catholic theologian, I propose to describe the sacramental community that embodies this faith and proclaims these values. I want to
talk about the Church, which as *Lumen gentium* makes clear remains
the one source of salvation for the whole world, including what we refer to as the "secular state."

In order to pursue this objective, it is important to recall that the
2000 Jubilee declaration *Christus Dominus* re-affirmed that "the distinction between *theological faith* and *belief* in the other religions must
be *firmly held*" (no. 7). Theological faith means the acceptance of the
truth revealed by the One and Triune God. Those who live according
to this faith and the charity that informs it are said to live the theologal life, from the French *la vie theologale*. The *Catechism of the Catholic Church* reintroduces the practice of referring to justified Christian
life as the "theologal" life.[1] Let me express my purpose in another way.
It is not my intention to reflect on religion and public life. We are not
in search of "first things" but of the First Thing, Who is First Truth
(Prima Veritas) itself. This lecture flows from what has been received
in faith from the One God who communicates, with infallible truthfulness, all that is required for salvation to the Church of Christ. I use
the word "flows" in the sense of depends on for its very being, as a river flows from its source or conclusions from a principle.

Specifically, I want to examine the ways that the divinely be-
stowed theologal life flourishes within the communion of the Church.
Christian moral realism accepts, to borrow a phrase from the lecture
of Daniel Robinson, that "the moral dimension of life is an integral
feature of how things are." The Christian moral realist further recognizes, however, that "how things are" is best discovered in the single
Church of Christ, which subsists in the Catholic Church, governed
by the Successor of Peter and by the Bishops in communion with

---

1. Specifically, the 1994 English version of the *Catechism (CCC)* speaks about the
"theologal path of our prayer" (no. 2607) and describes the first three petitions of the
Our Father as "more theologal" (no. 2803).

him.[2] Christian moral realism comprises doctrine, sacraments, and the moral life, especially the virtues that express new life in Christ. Moral realism in the Church is not restricted to establishing guidelines for ethical conduct. One confirmation of this assertion is found in the *Catechism,* which employs the term "theologal" to describe the way of life of those who give themselves over to contemplative prayer. Religion and prayer crown Christian moral realism. To appreciate the summit of moral realism, we must first examine its foundations. In order to understand the virtues of the Christian life, we must discover the matrices in which they flourish. The rest of this paper will examine the Christian virtues as they appear in each of the three vocations that distinguish the Church of Christ. Professor Kenneth Schmitz has already opened up for us the philosophical truth that helps us grasp what vocation in the Church supplies to the realization of Christian virtues. In summarizing his illuminating paper, "A Contemporary Philosophy of Action," Professor Schmitz says: "Now this means that a properly human act is not simply an outer performance, a behavior; it means rather that such action has an inner life as well." Where do we look for this "inner life" or maternal support for moral realism. I propose, again to borrow a phrase from Professor Schmitz, that to live at the center of the human drama is to dwell at the center of the Church.

Before discussing the vocations that mark the Church, allow me to establish the context for envisaging the concrete exercise of the theological virtues. Three theological coordinates govern a presentation of these divine energies. First, the threefold (triplex) grace of Christ: because "the one subject which operates in the two natures, human and divine, is the single Person of the Word" (*Dominus Jesus* no. 10), theologians have distinguished three graces that belong to Christ: the grace of the hypostatic union (the grace of the "single Person of the Word"), the grace resident in the human nature (Christ's

2. See Congregation for the Doctrine of the Faith, the declaration *Dominus Jesus* nos. 16–17.

own sanctifying or habitual grace), and the grace that overflows into the members of Christ (the capital or ecclesial or the grace of Headship). Second, because "the human virtues are rooted in the theological virtues, which adapt man's faculties for participation in the divine nature," there exist a specific form and dynamics of created grace: "for the theological virtues relate directly to God" (*CCC* no. 1812). Some theologians have construed man's capacity for God in an inclusive way; on their account, grace and nature are so intertwined as to make it difficult to speak about the "dynamics" of an uplifted life of supernatural grace. True Thomists take full account of the claim that the theological virtues "dispose Christians to live in a relationship with the Holy Trinity" (*CCC* no. 1812), and so are willing to talk about what is disposed. This leads to the third coordinate. Recall the foundational doctrine about creation, the doctrine of the *imago Dei*, man made in the image of God (see *CCC* nos. 1701–9, especially no. 1708 and no. 1709). It is possible to frustrate the *imago*. Creation is not redemption. In a word, the *imago Dei* can be actualized or frustrated depending on how we fulfill God's will for us. Directly related to this fundamental Christian tenet is the claim: "It must therefore be firmly believed as a truth of Catholic faith that the universal salvific will of the One and Triune God is offered and accomplished once for all in the mystery of the incarnation, death, and resurrection of the Son of God" (*Dominus Jesus* no. 14). The life of faith, hope, and charity establishes the believer in the communion of the Church. There he or she may dwell in one of three circles of ecclesial communion. We call them vocations: priesthood, consecrated life, and the lay state. We now turn to consider how these diverse vocations mediate the theologal life and those expressions of Christian moral realism that it supposes and perfects.

I. The mediation of the theologal life by priests

As we turn to consider the mediation of the vocations that distinguish the Church, we recognize that there are three circles of ecclesial communion that exist within the one communion of the Church: the presbyterate of the priests, the fraternity of the consecrated, and the family of the laity. Note that the Church does not envision a specific vocation as an isolated choice on the part of the believer; no, instead she insists that a vocation engage a pattern of reciprocal relationships. I call these distinctive relationships "circles of ecclesial communion." Because priests stand at the service of each circle, we first consider the priesthood and the presbyterate. The sacrament of priests brings a unique consecration or character. The spiritual identity of the priest governs the exercise of the sacred ministry confided to him at the time of ordination. The priest stands at the center of the Church as Head and Shepherd.

The mediation of the priest is first required in order for the Christian people to learn the dynamics of the theologal life. Look back at the great movements within the Church that rescued whole segments of the population from the disastrous cultural alternatives to accepting the Gospel, whether in uncivilized lands, such as the Jesuit missionaries to the North American frontier in the seventeenth century, or highly refined and advanced civilizations (societies), such as the spiritual renewal movements that started in Brittany and Normandy during the same period and extended into the eighteenth century. At the heart of such initiatives one always discovers holy priests. Recall the French cleric Louis Grignon de Montfort, whose spiritual instruction about and ardent devotion to the Blessed Virgin Mary remains a constant source of inspiration for the Church. This Missionary Apostolic, as Pope Clement XI designated him in 1706, illustrates the work that a priest must accomplish in an age of religious decline. De Montfort's theology has become associated with a robust Marian piety, but scholarly studies have shown that the saint's intuition encompassed the whole relationship between the Creator and the creature—the plan of divine Wisdom—and the special way in which the mediations that center on Christ and His Mother make it possible for the human creature to regain his proper status in the universe. Louis de Montfort instructed about the theologal life. He reminded his generation that "it is the internal quality of our actions that determine their human weight and their value," to cite again Professor Schmitz. The priest is able to encourage people to believe that this "internal quality" is made perfect only by a true and loving union with Jesus and Mary.

The diocesan priest embodies in a prima facie way the ideal of priestly service inasmuch as he finds himself immediately dependent on the Bishop of the particular Church and collaborates with him in the priestly office. Among the principal responsibilities that the priest receives by delegation from the Bishop is the authority to preach. Evangelization is a task that belongs to the whole Church, but preaching is reserved to those who participate in the "sacred power" of the priesthood, communicated through a valid Episcopate with Apostolic Succession. Preaching is a sacred action. It communicates to the world truths on which the world has no claim. The preacher must rely on what has been handed over to him. How else, as the Apostle reminds us, can one preach unless he has been commissioned? "And how are they to hear without a preacher? And how can men preach unless they are sent?" (Rom 10:14–15). Consider again the example of Saint Louis Grignon de Montfort: "The term 'apostolic' was a key word for Montfort. It properly described his 'missionary path.' Linked with the word 'missionary,' and having the etymological meaning of being 'sent,' it expressed something essential for St. Louis Marie."[3] We should also observe that "commission" meant a great deal to this ardent apostle of the theologal life. He walked from northwest France to Rome in order to receive from the Successor of Peter the designation and therefore the authority to undertake his missions.

What Louis de Montfort accomplished at the beginning of the eighteenth century, a Spanish priest had undertaken at the start of the thirteenth century. Dominic de Guzman also traveled to the Succes-

---

3. *Jesus Living in Mary: Handbook of the Spirituality of St. Louis Marie de Montfort* (Bayshore, N.Y.: Montfort Publications, 1994), p. 24.

sor of Peter, and received a similar mandate from Pope Honorious III to participate in the tasks that belong by divine right to the Bishops of the Church. It would be impossible to enumerate all of the other holy priests who have in one way or another taken up with seriousness the role of an apostolic missionary. We learn from the spirit of Saint Dominic that preaching issues forth best from a heart that is given over to praise and benediction: *laudare, benedicere, praedicare.* He reminds the priests of God's Church that if one is to communicate with enthusiasm and exactitude the truth of the Catholic religion, there exists no substitute for holiness of life. The spiritual adage *nemo potest dare quod non habet* captures the essence of this all-important truth. Church and world need priestly mediation more than ever during a period when people have been distracted from the important truths that define their creaturehood and thus their relation to God. How much of what goes on in the culture of death, the consumer society, the new paganism of especially Western culture shrouds a profound absence of what it means to be a creature? When we forget what it means to be a creature, then we can easily ignore the urgency of the theologal life. Only the Christian priest who stands between God and men as a mediator can restore, I would argue, the orders of nature and grace. To accomplish this task, he must become a father, a head, a shepherd, and never turn into just another religious functionary.[4]

The conciliar decree on priestly life and ministry *(Presbyterorum ordinis)* stipulates that priests are obliged to "share the truth of the Gospel" (no. 4) and, further, that the virtue of the priest, pastoral charity, be exercised by "accepting and putting into effect in a spirit of faith whatever is enjoined or recommended by the Supreme Pontiff and their own bishops" (no. 15). Number 16 of the same document sets forth what the Second Vatican Council teaches about the value of clerical celibacy: fuller consecration to Christ to whom priests are

---

4. Note what is taught in *Lumen gentium* no. 28: "It is in the Eucharistic cult or in the Eucharistic assembly of the faithful (synaxis) that they [priests] exercise in a supreme degree their office."

especially conformed; greater freedom to pursue the ministry of the Church, specifically "to accept a wider fatherhood in Christ"; and to point up the highest form of spousal love which is that discovered in the communion of the Church with God. *Pastores dabo vobis* especially develops the theme of spousal love and links it to the identity and virtue of the priest, pastoral charity. The "Oath of Fidelity," which is considered an official document of faith, asks pastors (and all clerics) to unite themselves with Bishops "as authentic doctors and teachers of the faith." It also enjoins that apostolic activity, especially preaching, which flows from the Church, not the individual, be carried out "in the communion of the same Church." Without this view of the ministry of especially the diocesan priest, it would be impossible to envisage a life of faith, which requires instruction; of hope, which requires encouragement; and of charity, which requires the exercise of Headship. In other words, without the ministry of priests, it is impossible to develop the theologal life.

To illustrate this point, let us consider the importance of preaching the truth about the moral virtues, especially chastity. Such virtue exists because reason is able to shape emotion. In *Summa theologiae* Ia q. 82, a. 4, ad 1, Aquinas observes that the "intellect penetrates the will with its act and object the way it does any other particular objects of understanding, like stone or wood, which all fall within the field of being and truth." Here we see the link between epistemological realism and moral realism. This principle, that intellect penetrates will as it does objects, governs the truth about sexual pleasure in the same way that it governs living by faith. The same intellect not only discriminates moral truths, for example, flesh to be cherished from flesh as abused, but it also penetrates faith truths, for example, God loves us because He is good and not because we are, Jesus saves us by his death on the cross, Mary is immaculately conceived, the sacraments are efficacious for our salvation, etc. Hence the Christian believer is able to choose, rationally, the truth of God's goodness, the power of the blood of Christ, the mediation of the Blessed Virgin Mary—in short, the whole economy of salvation—because faith penetrates the rational appetite with these good things. This shaping happens, however, only when the priest fulfills his *munus* within the Church. Moral realism requires a pulpit.[5]

How does the theologal life spill over into the affective life? Although the virtue of faith formally perfects the intellect, it motivates the virtue of hope whereby the believer clings to God's omnipotent mercy as the source of salvation. This spiritual clinging forms the basis for the whole Christian life. It responds to the many places in the New Testament where Jesus encourages his disciples to remain closely united with him and with his Heavenly Father. Furthermore, the believer can make this efficacious choice through the intellectual appetite even in the face of a whole range of disordered sense appetites which may, depending on his state of personal growth and development, overwhelm his sense powers, internal and external, at a given moment. Growth in Christian moral virtue requires that a person be instructed in how to make this kind of act of faith. One preamble is essential. To enter effectively into the mystery of Christ's love requires being practically convinced that God loves the human creature because He is good and not because He finds something lovable in the creature. Without the knowledge that God loves only the good that he himself creates, a person would most likely give up in despair when faced with the challenges to living the moral life. Such a one would falsely conclude that even though salvation is promised, holiness of life is elusive. This sort of outlook leaves a person with no exit. Or, to cite the metaphors that Professor Schmitz finds attractive, this person moves along without flowers, or lights, or salt. Many people, desirous of loving God, are blackmailed by a false understanding of the divine generosity. God loves us because He is good, not because we are.

5. Rev. Jeremy Guilbeau completed in 2002 a master's thesis at Saint John's Seminary on the contribution of an English Benedictine to the renewal of Catholicism during the period following the re-establishment of the Hierarchy in England: "'Hidden in the Quiver of God': Bishop John Cuthbert Hedley on Priestly Formation for Preaching."

Future research at the Institute and elsewhere will help psychologists and theologians better to grasp the significance of the distinction between the two kinds of appetites operative in the human person. To distinguish clearly between the rational (or intellectual) and sense appetites affords Aquinas a way to affirm the ultimate triumph of God's power over fallen nature. When Aquinas asks whether the irascible and concupiscible appetites obey reason, he concludes that the sense appetites obey reason because particular truths can both calm wrath and fear or arouse them and, furthermore, that they obey the will since human action requires the "consensus" of the higher appetite. Although philosophers are familiar with the anthropological principles at work in this affirmation, I believe that to speak this way could appear naive to psychologists and perhaps others who encounter so much emotional disorder. Does the priest as priest enjoy a place in an institute dedicated to the psychological sciences? I think so. Who else is able to proclaim authoritatively that the ultimate truths that control the appetites are revealed truths? To gainsay this startling affirmation is to run afoul of what Aquinas says about the man without grace: "*Sed quod diu maneat absque peccato mortali, esse non potest.*"[6] It will take some time, however, for modern psychology to overcome its prejudices and warm to the idea of revealed religion. To live the theologal life, which includes the infused moral virtues, a person must accept in faith the person and teaching of Jesus Christ and the whole economy of salvation. This act of faith enables a person to achieve a "consensus" (to use a technical term for harmony) in the will that disposes him or her to choose the good. The Christian believer maintains this harmony by maintaining a union with Jesus Christ in the Church of faith and sacraments. This affective union that lies at the heart of the theologal life, it should be clear, depends on the mediation that occurs only through the sacred ministry of priests.

---

6. "But it cannot be that he remains for a long time without mortal sin." *Summa theologiae* Ia-IIae q. 109, a. 8.

II. *The witness to the theologal life by consecrated persons*

The fraternity of consecrated life offers a refreshing alternative to the isolation that envelops the modern individual, whose monad-like existence is oddly prefigured in the way that resembles how the eighteenth-century thinker Leibnitz imagined the concursus of human and divine freedom. The paradox of individualism is perhaps most realized in the culture that the United States has spawned since the end of the Second World War. The more people strive to guarantee individual liberties, the more they find themselves isolated and alone, and thus inclined to substitute ersatz forms of being-together for true community. To the brilliant and in-depth analysis that Professor Paul Vitz gives in his "From the Modern Individual to the Transmodern Person," I would like to add the political enthusiasm for recognizing same-sex unions to the list of indicators that we need to develop his transmodern personalism. In the Church of today, consecrated persons must remind a generation of lost individuals that truth itself and the truth about friendship remain the only goods that authentically perfect the human person. The *communio* of the Church affords the only guaranteed form of inclusiveness, to borrow the neologism that dominates so much of our public rhetoric. Within the *communio* of the Church, there exists a special form of communion whose intensity best represents the original coming-together in the upper room, where the Apostles united with Mary, the Mother of Jesus, received the parted tongues of fire that signaled a divine renewal of the whole face of the earth.

The lived witness of the evangelical counsels offers to the Church a constant reminder of the radical nature of Christian conversion. One can adapt to our present circumstances the explanations that classical spiritual authors gave for advancing religious consecration. We can say that poverty opposes everything that is corrupt in the culture of consumption; chastity, everything that is disordered in the culture of permissiveness; and obedience, everything that is distorted in the assumption (which goes unchallenged in the politics of secular liberalism) that power constitutes the only worthwhile human reality. In order best to examine how consecrated life blesses the Church, we should consider its prototypical realization, which is the monastery. Classical forms of monastic life are scarce these days. In the United States, we now have Our Lady of Clear Creek, the new American daughter house of the French Benedictine Abbey of Fontgombault, which belongs to the Solemnes Congregation. This new monastery is located outside Tulsa, Oklahoma.

It is interesting to observe that twentieth-century North American Catholicism, especially after the Second World War, when expansion to the suburbs proceeded at a rapid pace, may be the first time in the history of Christianity when many members of the Church have had to survive without enjoying some proximity to a monastery. For reasons that can be traced to historical occurrences in Europe (when hostilities against the Church prevailed), as well as to the need of the immigrant Catholic community, this circumstance was not so apparent in the nineteenth century: witness the Franciscan missions in California and especially the great Benedictine monasteries that grew up alongside the pioneer Church in the Midwest and Northwest. Today, however, only a very small percentage of American Catholics know about and are able to experience monastic life; indeed absent to them is any formal representation of religious life—such as was provided for them in the great urban centers of the Northeast by Redemptorists, Passionists, and Franciscans. Without a monastery—and now I use the term in the broad and analogical sense—can the Church protect herself against the adverse influences on the members of her community of a secular culture that so profoundly lacks a sense of interrelatedness? When one considers the Trinitarian structure of the theologal life, the question may be put differently: "How can the theologal life flourish apart from the witness of a monastery?"

If I understand the best of transmodern personalism, the argument is advanced that interrelatedness ensures a person's contact with reality. Individualism, on the other hand, removes "people from reality, from the external world created by God and filled with real others."[7] Removal from God makes it psychologically difficult for a person to practice the most essential of Christian virtues, namely, confidence. By observing a rule and practicing lawful obedience, the monk or nun encourages people to trust in the paternal providence of God. Perhaps no more compelling analogy comes from the lips of our blessed Savior than what he speaks in the Gospel of Matthew: "If you, with all your sins, know how to give your children what is good, how much more will your heavenly Father give good things to anyone who asks him!" (Mt 7:12). Every Christian needs to be reminded of this lesson that only the Church conserves. Confidence in the providence of God forms the foundation for the everyday living out of Christian faith. In the period after the Council, some theologians began to interpret the value of evangelical obedience in terms of creating a disposition in the members of religious institutes for a more effective deployment of their corporate talents. These theorists missed the point of what religious profession or consecration accomplishes in the Church. The religious observes a life of obedience in order to show that obedience remains foundational to the way of every Christian vocation. It is symptomatic, perhaps, of the kind of spiritual renewal needed today in the Church that the documents that come forth from the Roman Curia have found it opportune repeatedly to stress the "obedience of faith" (Rom 1:5), which is how the Apostle Paul defines his own ministry: "Jesus Christ our Lord, through whom we have received grace and apostleship to bring about the obedience of faith for the sake of his name among all the nations . . ." (Rom 1:4–5).

The flourishing of consecrated life in the Church as well as the various ways in which the classical forms of religious consecration have been adapted to suit the needs of the present time remind us of the

---

7. Paul C. Vitz, "From the Modern Individual to the Transmodern Person," ch. 5 in the present volume.

importance of conversion of life. Without *conversio,* there is no the-ologal life. The Desert Fathers introduced the *conversio morum* into the vocabulary of their disciples. These stressed how much what is of the world needs to be left behind when one comes into the school of discipleship that the Lord has established for his beloved. The Second Vatican Council's emphasis on the universal call to holiness signals that the Church abides at the heart of the world. Everything she does draws toward the center. The spirituality of the Council, to coin an expression, excludes a one-sided emphasis on secularity, such as occurred in some quarters in the 1970s. One can still retreat from the world, even while remaining in the world to sanctify it. Some have been slow, however, to recognize this truth ever old and ever new. Father Matthew Lamb of Boston College has illustrated in a compelling way that those who interpreted the Council's teaching, especially with the theretofore unavailable assistance of the mass media, skewed the authentic teaching of the Council. These popularizers, as Father Lamb calls them, introduced an erroneous view of the relationship between the Church and the world from which the Church is only now recovering, slowly. A conflation occurred that obscured the special rhythms of the theologal life. The decline in so many religious institutes of women in the United States surely finds part of its explanation in this mistaken interpretation of what the Fathers of the Second Vatican Council had hoped to communicate about the "perfection of charity."

Consecrated chastity possesses its own specific objective within the communion of the Church. It is important to distinguish consecrated chastity from the promise of chaste celibacy. By their virginity, religious, and especially religious women, and among them most especially cloistered religious women, reveal the character of the Church as *Verbi Sponsa.* It may be difficult to formulate a mental picture of some religious as "Brides," for example, the dogsled missionaries in the Arctic region of North America. And yet by their whole-hearted commitment to the work of evangelization, even these men of gnarled and leathery complexion demonstrate what it means for the Church to focus everything on the coming of the Lord. Because it allowed the Christian to fulfill completely the one thing that is necessary, Saint Paul, as we know, urged virginity for the sake of the Kingdom: "I mean, brethren, the appointed time has grown very short" (1 Cor 7:29). To this injunction, we should also add the accumulated wisdom of the Church which Aquinas repeats: "sexual pleasure withdraws the soul from that perfect disposition of tending toward God" (*Summa theologiae* IIa-IIae q. 186, a. 4). In the Church, the witness of consecrated religious, especially the women who give themselves night and day to the worship of God, to prayer, and to cultivating the divine friendship, reminds each baptized person that he or she must remain clean of heart, with a mind fully centered on the Lord whose Church we inhabit in charity. The theologal life finds its eminent expression in consecrated, especially contemplative, life. In a word, there we find hearts transformed by the Lord. No wonder that in his postsynodal exhortation addressed to them the Holy Father places consecrated persons on Mount Tabor, the Mount of the Transfiguration.

III. Christ's lay faithful and the work of evangelization: spread of the theologal life

Priesthood and consecrated persons are vocations of service and witness. Those who follow these vocations represent a small percentage of the numbers that constitute the Church. For reasons that include the continuation of the human race, the vast majority of Christian believers discover their vocation and their holiness as laity. Recall the important and specific charge that the Second Vatican Council has given to Christ's lay faithful. These Christian men and women realize their vocation when they discharge their unique obligation to transform and sanctify the *saeculum*. While this mandate is a well-known one, some serious misunderstandings about the proper place of the laity in the Church still exist, especially in the countries dominated by German and Anglo-American theology. Because of a series of complex theological and social factors, the full recovery of the secular vocation of the laity has not been achieved. In many parts of the country, I have been struck by the ways in which an elision is made from receiving certain tasks, such as teaching and liturgical duties, and becoming personally identified as a Catholic who performs those tasks. The philosophical explanation lies, in my judgment, in the cultural proclivity to replace office *(munus)* and personal identity with a self-definition based on role and task. Because there exists no pre-Enlightenment culture in the United States, there is very little to remind a citizen of this country of his "status," which is such an indispensable part of Christian revelation about who we are. All members of the Church must appropriate the authentic teaching of the Council, and resist the Protestantization of the Church that four centuries after the Reform of the sixteenth century once again threatens to undermine the fundamental reality of the Church and her mission of sanctifying, teaching, and governing. The fruits of the Catholic Reform of the post-Tridentine period still remind us of the need to provide for the People of God clear and accurate guidance about how they sanctify the world.

Professor Robert George has observed that "despite the fact that public morality is a public good, its maintenance depends much more on contributions of private institutions than on those of law and government." His paper on the concept of public morality opens out to the Christian vocation of the laity. The People of God live according to the spirit of the new dispensation, which is the inner grace of the Holy Spirit. External conformity only realizes half the grace of the Holy Spirit. Such observance never exhausts the theologal life. The full power of the new dispensation, of what Jesus introduces through the Paschal Mystery, informs every fiber of the human being. The "new man" of which Christian revelation speaks is the person transformed from the inside out. Without this kind of transformation, there is little hope that the People of God will be able to do all that their distinctive vocation in the Church requires of them. Interiority cannot be taught unless it is lived. Each person must show to the Church a living proof of that charity and unity that distinguishes the Church of Christ. The theologal life flows from the Eucharist. As Saint Paul reminded the Corinthians: "Because there is one bread, we who are many are one body, for we all partake of the one bread" (1 Cor 10:17). Saint Augustine's exclamation in his commentary on John's Gospel becomes for the laity a warrant, a duty to de discharged, a sacred trust to be lived interiorly: "Sacrament of piety, sign of unity, bond of charity!"[8] Because the Eucharist is the sacrament and source of ecclesial unity, the laity join consecrated persons gathered around the Bishop and his priests in the one communion of the Church. From this experience of Christ's love, each member of the Body moves out to sanctify, diversely, the world.

The lay ecclesial movements offer encouragement, though like each new stirring of the Holy Spirit, they require time to find a precise point of insertion into the Church's hierarchical structure. Ecclesial movements offer to the People of God significant means to live out their vocations. It is important for us to recall that each of these movements provides a structured and organized program for spiritual formation. This program extends not only to initial formation, but also includes permanent formation. We are reminded of the earliest designation for the Christian life, namely, that it forms a "Way." The pastors of the Church should appreciate the spiritual formation that authentic lay movements give to the lay faithful. In my experience, the lay movements provide one of the few sources of authentic Catholic spirituality for Catholics today, since much of what passes for spiritual theology or spirituality, at least in the United States, is not sufficiently informed by Catholic doctrine, and at times becomes too much informed by secular if not pagan resources. It may come as a source of some surprise to learn that the Bishops of the United States

8. *In Johannis Evangelium* 26:13.

are experiencing resistance from Catholics in their effort to persuade people away from certain spiritual exercises which have no known connection to any Christian tradition. The theologal life is defined by the theological virtues, not by whatsoever attempt to rejoice the human spirit. Psychological studies informed by the faith can develop critical evaluations of proposed recipes for wellness and other notions that promote pseudo-spiritual development. This objective suggests another task to set before the Institute for the Psychological Sciences.

Since the Second Vatican Council, we have become accustomed to ponder deeply on the relationship of *missio* and *communio*. The encyclical letter *Redemptoris missio* has helped the whole Church grasp and deal with the configuration of mission that confronts her in the third Christian millennium. Because the Church is missionary by her nature, it is fair to say that every member serves the Church's missionary mandate. The sacramental mediation of the Church achieves a certain transcendence when the Church reaches out as a sacrament of salvation to every human being on the planet. We know the special circumstances that prompted in 2000 the issuance of the declaration *Dominus Jesus*. The truths of Catholic and divine faith that are recalled in that succinct catechism of essential Catholic doctrine possess a special meaning for the "missionary." No human person should be left to worship God in a way that does not allow for a full and active participation in the Eucharistic synaxis. The theologal life is sustained during this moment of participation in the Eucharist.[9]

The Church's missionary mandate—of her *missio ad gentes*—leads one to reflect on inculturation. Recall the Church's missionary efforts in China in the seventeenth and eighteenth centuries. Historians in-

---

9. The Second Vatican Council explicitly recognized the spiritual distress that results from a paucity of priests in a given region when it urged Bishops that "they should take special care of those regions of the world in which the word of God is yet to be proclaimed or in which, mainly because of lack of priests, the faithful are in grave danger of falling away from the moral standards of Christian life and even of losing the faith itself" (*Christus Dominus* no. 6).

terpret the Rites Controversy differently, but the general, especially Protestant, view has been to consider the episode a damaging one. The distinguished Lutheran theologian George Lindbeck, who had been an ecumenical observer at the Second Vatican Council and is himself the son of Protestant missionaries to China, holds a different account of what happened. Whereas many thought the action of the Holy See impeded the growth of Christianity in China, the fact is that what the Popes of the eighteenth century did actually ensured that the Gospel of Christ would flourish among people of every class and station. The proposals for adaptation to the culture of the Chinese may have been discerned as authentic Christianity by those who were well instructed and of the upper class, but for the rice farmer and the fisherman, the housewife and the spinster, the sophistication of the adaptations had made it difficult for them fully to comprehend that anything different was at work. These folk would have missed what makes Christian life and worship new. In other words, the People of God would not have recognized the "definitive and complete character of the revelation of Jesus Christ" (*Dominus Jesus* no. 5). We return to the importance of the sacramental mediation of the Church, and of the definitive form that the theologal life takes within this communion. This form of Christian life cannot unfold without proper liturgical rites. Strategies for inculturation should neither obscure the truth of the Gospel nor transmogrify the Catholic religion.

The Church confides to the lay person the work of the evangelization. This witness requires a renewal of spirit. Each one must ask for the grace to enjoy a deeper love of the mysteries of the faith that he or she celebrates. Christians must do everything to ensure that the Church of faith and sacraments reaches the farthest corners of the globe, and this can happen only to the extent that we ourselves live these gifts of grace. Missionary zeal always characterizes the saints. One thinks first of all of Saint Francis Xavier and the flood of enthusiasm for evangelization that he unleashed, but also of Saint Francis of Assisi and Saint Dominic Guzman, both of whom cherished never fully realized desires to carry out the *missio ad gentes*. The modern period affords examples of men and, especially, of women too numerous to mention who have taken up this example. The missionary desires of contemplatives, like Therese of Lisieux, also serve to encourage and strengthen the Church. The bipolarity of monastics and missionaries, to borrow a designation from Hans Urs von Balthasar, will always serve as a mark of the true Church. Between these categories, lay persons find their mission. The Church can never forget the ordering of the Joyful Mysteries of the Rosary: the Annunciation and the Visitation. The first thing that the embryonic Jesus does is travel, in the womb of his Mother, whose embrace of her cousin Elizabeth establishes Mary forever as the Cause of Our Joy, *Causa nostrae latitiae*.

"In a word, you must be perfected as your heavenly Father is perfect" (Mt 5:48). The Christian Gospel is transformative. Well has Don Luigi Guisanni reminded us that the Gospel introduces the believer into a "school of discipleship." Growth in discipleship occurs according to the vocation that each one has received. Earlier I referred to a foundational principle of Christian discipleship, something that the theology of Saint Thomas Aquinas teaches with special clarity: God loves us because He is good, not because we are. Since there exists no other motive for divine love other than God's own goodness, human freedom is most free when it is subordinated to the divine initiative. Because the creature is dependent on God, our goodness belongs first of all to God in a way that never diminishes the dignity of human freedom. On the contrary, as the saints remind us over and over again, the one who lives more fully in God becomes who he is. This man or woman achieves the freedom that ennobles. It is, as Aquinas again taught the Church, a freedom for excellence. The concrete name for this specifically Christian excellence is the theologal life.

Nothing that happens for good in the Church affects only the one who accomplishes the good deed. The Mystical Body, as we know, is related in such a way that wherever charity increases in one, so charity increases in the other members—in ways known only to God, to be sure, but in real and measurable ways, nonetheless. A person's own renewal in charity, one's own re-dedication to prayer and spiritual discipline, our own re-commitment to our specific work not only benefit the other members of the Church in the invisible workings of the Mystical Body, but also in the visible workings of the Body which is the Church. When each of the three circles of ecclesial communion virtuously work together, the world is won back for moral realism. Not the moral realism of the philosophers, but the moral realism of the Eucharist. From the Holy Communion, each member returns to his or her work renewed in confidence. Without the Church of Christ, there would be no flourishing of human virtue in the "secular state." This is not a lesson new to the Christian people. They learned it first from the pen of Saint Augustine. Neither person nor polis flourish outside of Christ. From the very beginning of her existence, the Church has sought to shape the city, the kingdom, the regime, the state, the society, the culture. There is no such thing, however, as a purely supernatural activity. Grace builds on nature. The Institute for the Psychological Sciences aims to examine the intersection of these two God-given endowments in the place where spirit and grace meet. The analysis will require care and precision. In the end, however, the dialogue between theology and the psychological sciences promises great success for both person and polis, believer and Church.

CONTRIBUTORS

Hadley Arkes is Edward N. Ney Professor of Jurisprudence and American Institutions at Amherst College. His main interests as a writer and a teacher have been focused on political philosophy, public policy, and constitutional law. In those areas, he has written several books, including *The Philosopher in the City* (1981), *First Things* (1986), *Beyond the Constitution* (1990), *The Return of George Sutherland* (1994), and *Natural Rights and the Right to Choose* (2002). His writings have also appeared in the *Wall Street Journal*, *Commentary*, the *Washington Post*, the *Weekly Standard*, *National Review*, and *First Things*.

Romanus Cessario is professor of theology at St John's Seminary in Brighton, Massachusetts, and director of several research projects at the Institute for the Psychological Sciences. His doctoral studies were at the University of Fribourg, in Switzerland. Father Cessario has written several books and many articles in moral theology, including *The Moral Virtues and Theological Ethics* (1991), *Christian Faith and the Theological Life* (1996), *Introduction to Moral Theology* (2001), *The Virtues or the Examined Life* (2002), and *A Short History of Thomism* (2005); and is co-editor of *Veritatis Splendor and the Renewal of Moral Theology* (1999).

Robert P. George is the McCormick Professor of Jurisprudence at Princeton University and an internationally recognized authority on constitutional law and legal philosophy. A graduate of Harvard Law School, Professor George holds a doctorate in legal philosophy from Oxford University. He is the author of *Making Men Moral: Civil Liberties and Public Morality* (1993), *In Defense of Natural Law* (1999), and *The Clash of Ortho-*

doxies: Law, Religion and Morality in Crisis (2001); and editor of *Natural Law Theory: Contemporary Essays* (1992), *The Autonomy of Law: Essays on Legal Positivism* (1996), *Natural Law, Liberalism, and Morality* (1996), *Natural Law and Moral Inquiry* (1998), *Great Cases in Constitutional Law* (2000), *Natural Law and Public Reason* (2000), and *The Meaning of Marriage: Family, State, Market, and Morals* (2006).

Michael Novak, theologian, author, and former U.S. ambassador, holds the George Frederick Jewett Chair in Religion, Philosophy, and Public Policy at the American Enterprise Institute in Washington, D.C. His writings have appeared in every major Western language, and in Bengali, Korean, and Japanese. He has written more than twenty-five books, including *On Cultivating Liberty: Reflections on Moral Ecology* (1999), *A Free Society Reader* (2000), *On Two Wings: Humble Faith and Common Sense at the American Founding* (2001), *Three in One: Essays on Democratic Capitalism 1976–2000* (2001), *Universal Hunger for Liberty: Why the Clash of Civilizations Is Not Inevitable* (2004), *Washington's God* (2006), and his renowned *The Spirit of Democratic Capitalism* (1982).

Daniel N. Robinson is distinguished research professor at Georgetown University, faculty fellow in philosophy at Oxford University, and visiting professor at the Institute for the Psychological Sciences. He is editor of the *Journal of Theoretical & Philosophical Psychology.* Over the years, through books, articles, and lectures, Professor Robinson has contributed to the literature in philosophy of mind, philosophy of science, intellectual history, philosophy of law, ethics, and the basic sciences. His books include *Aristotle's Psychology* (1989), *An Intellectual History of Psychology* (1995), *Wild Beasts and Idle Humors* (1996), and *Praise and Blame: Moral Realism and Its Applications* (2002); and he is co-editor of numerous volumes, including *The Mind* (1998).

Kenneth L. Schmitz is professor of philosophy at the John Paul II Institute for Studies on Marriage and Family in Washington, D.C., and professor emeritus of philosophy at Trinity College, University of Toronto. He is the author of *The Gift: Creation* (1982), *At the Center of the Human Drama: The Philosophical Anthropology of Karol Wojtyla / Pope John Paul II* (1993), and *The Recovery of Wonder: The New Freedom and the Asceticism of Power* (2005).

Craig Steven Titus is research professor at the Institute for the Psychological Sciences, and research and teaching fellow in the Department of Moral Theology and Ethics, University of Fribourg, in Switzerland. He has written *Resilience and the Virtue of Fortitude: Aquinas in Dialogue with the Psychological Sciences* (2006) and co-edited *The Pinckaers Reader: Renewing Thomistic Moral Theology* (2005).

Paul C. Vitz is professor and senior scholar at the Institute for the Psychological Sciences. For many years, he was professor of psychology at New York University. He received his doctorate at Stanford University. Dr. Vitz's work is focused on the development of a Christian approach to psychology, breaking away from the trends of secular humanism prevalent today. He has written numerous books, including *Modern Art and Modern Science: The Parallel Analysis of Vision* (1984), *Sigmund Freud's Christian Unconscious* (1993), *Psychology as Religion: The Cult of Self Worship* (1977, 1994), and *Faith of the Fatherless: The Psychology of Atheism* (2000). He has also co-edited *The Self: Beyond the Postmodern Crisis* (2006).

INDEX OF SUBJECTS

tal, 122, 125, 142n, 146, 149, 151, 156–57, 159. *See also* sexuality

relativism, 38–40, 46, 71, 78, 80, 113, 117–18, 130

religion, 2, 4–5, 12–14, 20, 23, 63, 114, 126, 132, 140–52, 154–55, 159, 162, 171, 176–77

Republicans, 94–97, 99–101, 142n

responsibility, 5–6, 8, 11, 16, 33, 35–36, 58–59, 73

reward(s), 7, 21, 43–45

rights, 69–72, 82, 104, 106, 152; human, 33, 84, 144, 146, 152; natural, 78, 84–85, 107, 146, 149, 175; right/wrong, 40–41, 64, 68, 79, 84–85, 107

Roe v. Wade, 99n

rosary, 24, 172

sacrament(s), 15, 155, 157, 160, 162, 169–71

salvation, 154, 160–62, 170

sanctification, 15, 156, 166–69. *See also* holiness

science(s), 16, 46–47, 51, 110, 152; human, 1–4, 88, 162, 170, 173, 175–77; philosophy of, 47, 52n, 176

Second Vatican Council, 15, 29–30, 33, 72, 159, 166–67, 170–71

Second World War, 163–64

secular state, 1–2, 154, 173

self, 11–2, 31–3, 109–31; enlightened self-interest, 13, 134n, 137–9; independent, 114, 118, 122, 125, 127; self-development, 12, 71, 110–14, 119, 121, 125, 131; self-government, 13, 133, 144, 151–52

sentiment(s), moral, 6, 38, 40–43. *See also* emotion(s)

sexuality, 30, 56–57, 59, 66, 110, 119, 142n, 160, 167; same-sex relations, 59, 163; vice, 9–10, 66–68, 70, 100. *See also* morality, sexual

sociology, 46, 50

sodomy, 74

spirituality, 2, 4–5, 18, 24, 118, 129, 152, 157–59, 161, 163, 165–66, 169–70, 173

state (government), 8, 13, 22, 60–65, 71–74, 90–92, 133, 135, 137–41, 151, 154, 173. *See also* government

Stenberg v. Carhart, 92

subject, human, 5, 26–27, 31, 39, 46, 50–51, 155

Summa contra gentiles, 141

Summa theologiae, 73, 140, 160, 162, 167

technology, 20, 34, 114–15

theology, ii, 1, 4, 14, 26–27, 120–23, 128, 140, 153–73; of the body, 30, 120–21n

therapy, 2, 112–13, 115–16, 118n, 126

Thomism, 127, 137, 156, 175

tradition, 25, 37, 47, 67–68, 73, 99; Judeo-Christian, 13–14, 118, 120, 153; philosophical, 103, 121, 124, 127; psychological 53, 115, 124; religious 13, 120–21, 139, 145, 170

transcendence, 2, 25, 36, 118, 122, 129, 170

trust, 150–51, 165

truth(s), 3, 6, 36, 149, 152; claims, 49, 80; moral, 54, 84–85, 106–7, 160, 162–63; perfective power of, 36, 163; theological, 15, 153–56, 158–60, 162–63, 171

tyranny, 5, 13, 23, 26, 135–36n, 148

unconscious, 12, 30, 36, 110–12, 177

understanding, moral, 45–46, 48, 58, 84, 103

utilitarianism, 11, 26–27, 98, 103, 137, 149

value(s), 18, 20, 28, 35–38, 40, 45, 50, 53, 114–15, 142n; and fact, 7, 47, 49, 53n; and faith, 1–2, 13–14, 153–54, 158–59; of the human person, 13, 27, 35, 146–47

Verbi sponsa, 166

vice(s), 8–10, 39, 67–69, 72–74, 147, 151

virtue(s), 8–10, 14, 39, 46, 58–59, 66, 72, 77, 128; Christian, 14–15, 155–56, 159–62, 165, 170, 173; moral, 15, 73, 130, 160; promotion of, 8–9, 72–73, 160

vocation(s), 155, 157, 165, 167–69, 172

voluntarism, 13, 135

Watergate, 101

welfare state, 13, 62–63, 137

Zabar's v. Virginia, 82

INDEX OF NAMES

The Person and the Polis: Faith and Values within the Secular State was designed and typeset by Kachergis Book Design of Pittsboro, North Carolina. It was printed on 60-pound Natural Offset and bound by McNaughton & Gunn of Saline, Michigan.